RAINBOW WEATHER

stories
_{from a}
beautiful
nowhere

Kat Koch

Library of Congress Control Number: 2025903604

ISBN: PB: 979-8-9926805-0-8   EBOOK: 979-8-9926805-1-5

Manuscript Evaluation by Natasha Fracchiolla, Leanne Crighton, Candice Burnett and Robyn Porteous.

Copy Editing by Jaime Conway

Book Cover by Megan Clancy

Interior Design and Maps by Liesel Blendulf

Author's Photograph by Shay Hunston

First edition 2025

"Hearts don't actually break, but sometimes they're forced to grow so fast, it feels like they have."

-Unknown

For

Jean Williams – so much time, so little to do.

Deanna Tregoning – inhale, exhale, thank you.

Women of all ages – if you feel the call to travel, please go. It may be scary at times, but I promise, it will be worth it.

Tim Selim – you were right. When I am an old woman, I won't regret my time in Ireland.

And finally, to the people of West Cork – thank you.

Contents

A Foreword by Tim Selim

S kydive.

Fly a plane. Scuba dive. Rebuild a classic motorcycle. Learn to play the fiddle. Visit New England in Autumn. Make a potato gun. Read the classics. Get eyes on the great pyramids and wander around South America; preferably on a motorcycle.

These are just a handful of the items I wrote on my bucket list in a finely made leather bound journal. I found it recently in an antique bookcase I have that houses my most precious books. The darkly tanned leather book-ended the top shelf of titles and camouflaged itself against the stained wood rendering it practically invisible.

I made that bucket list with Kat decades ago, under an umbrella of moss and lichen covered trees in the Pacific Northwest. I feel compelled to confess she was the inspiration and the instigator. And I'm so glad we did.

The first and only time I went scuba diving and blissed out watching air bubbles from my regulator mingle with a coral reef in the Caribbean Sea remains one of the most vivid memories I retain. I'd also encourage anyone not to underestimate how much good clean fun can be had by building and utilising a potato gun.

That being said, the vast majority of the dozens of entries on my bucket list lack a check mark next to them. I, like many, if not most people, spend more time thinking about adventuring and expanding my horizons than actually doing it.

Then there's Kat.

Be careful what you say to Kat. If you're standing next to the ocean on a cold rainy day with her, the surf bustling enough to be concerning, and you say 'It'd be awesome to body surf right now' you will end up in that chilly water in a matter of seconds. No wetsuit? No problem. Birthday suit. Her enthusiasm is contagious and unwavering.

Hiking with Kat is an experience. It's not so much like walking on the trail less travelled. It's like, trail? What fun is that? Swamps won't stop her. She'll crawl through thickets in the dark. She'll get to the mountain top if she feels like it but also might have a magical and prolonged encounter with a grandmother tree and scrap the whole agenda altogether. It's not a lack of focus. It's a focus on the adventure, the expansion, the possibilities, instead of a focus on the status quo.

Her travels aren't superficial encounters with landscapes and people. They are simultaneously spiritual and educational experiences. Her journey on ayahuasca excluded; they are usually sober examinations of consciousness, purpose, history, and all the big questions in life that many of us shun in our day to day lives.

Her ancestral heritage drew her to the motherland; Ireland. When she moved there it seemed to me like it happened suddenly, but in reality, it was a monumental effort of logistics to overcome the challenges of opening a new chapter of her life in Europe. During the years she lived there she fit right in with her red hair and gift of gab. The emerald isle seemed to welcome her. My Irish genes perked up whenever she shared stories of her time there exploring the people, the culture, the land, and the sea. Regardless of your lineage, her writing will encourage you to connect with it.

If, like me, you find as you've aged the idea of long TSA lines and 16 hour flights in coach are a formidable deterrent to traveling, and you have a little anxiety about uprooting and diving into a new culture, this book is for you. If you're a bit bogged down by the business of living; jobs, kids, dogs, bills and all the other adulting that sucks the life out of us sometimes, this book is for you. If you've always thought about going to Ireland someday, or anywhere for that matter, this book will inspire you. You'll see that adventure can take any form and never has to stop. Child-like curiosity and wonder will seem possible again. You'll definitely laugh. Live vicariously through Kat for a while, as I've had the pleasure of doing. You won't regret it.

Lastly, if you're ever lucky enough to meet her in person, ask her to sing.

Preface

I decided to move to Ireland in a graveyard.

I used to go to this one near my house and sit under a Western Red Cedar tree. Sometimes I'd bring a journal and write. And sometimes I'd wander between the gravestones. Who were these people? And why did I feel such a sense of peace here? Most of the living people I knew were a little bit afraid of them, and of me being in them if I'm honest. I guess I just felt differently. To me, they felt simple. Peaceful. Calm.

My decision to move wasn't an easy one. I struggled with it. And I couldn't place why I was having such an internal conflict.

The summer before the move, I travelled to Ireland and could not get it out of my mind and heart that I wanted to relocate. I was absolutely in love with the place. All my trips were full of fun and inspiring experiences. I was learning something new all the time, and immersing myself in a culture that was so different to my own. I couldn't get enough. At that time, I'd been running a yearly retreat there for a few seasons; so this idea had been brewing for a while.

That summer my mom joined me for part of my trip, and we headed up the country to County Mayo, basing ourselves in Louisburgh, near Ireland's holiest mountain. One night, I'd just gotten off the phone with my best friend Tim back in the States. We'd exchanged stories of our delicious confusions, him about a current relationship and me, about my hope and fear around moving abroad. I could see the bright, full moon peeking in through the curtains, so I walked outside to get some fresh air. I'm pretty sure the moon called me; she and I were talking a lot back then.

I let the moonlight wash over me, through me, deep into my bones. It felt so good. I closed my eyes. I could hear the waves rolling up and out, up and out on the pebble beach. Each time a wave rolled in it sounded like the rush of a thousand marbles. And each time it rolled out that sound magnified twofold.

As I stood, I felt the uncertainty and internal wrestling about "to move or not to move" subside. And out of nowhere, this empowering peace filled my whole body. Just like the moonlight had done. I suddenly knew that everything would be okay, no matter what happened, and I let myself soak in that message, glowing as I soaked. It is still one of the top ten most beautiful energy moments of my life.

The feeling stayed with me till morning, when I dove again, back into the Sea of Uncertainty and continued wrestling with the waves of myself.

A few weeks later I flew home to Western Washington. I broke up with my boyfriend, a decision I'd also been wrestling with, and moved into Tim's house. It was there, as I tried to make a clear decision, the clarity finally came.

And it came in the form of a Carlos Castaneda quote. When I read it, I instantly knew where some of my struggles had been coming from!

"Then ask yourself and yourself alone this one question. Does this path have heart? All paths are the same. They lead nowhere. They are paths going through the brush or into the brush or under the brush of the Universe. The only question is: Does this path have heart? If it does, then it is a good path. If it doesn't, then it is of no use."

- The Teachings of Don Juan: A Yaqui Way of Knowledge

I've since come to learn that the original quote is written differently, though the message is the same. But it didn't matter. It was exactly how I needed to hear it.

For the first time in my adult life, I had two decisions before me and *both* of them had heart. I could go either way. To Ireland. Or stay in the Pacific Northwest. Both had heart. And somehow, with the choice before me, no more right or wrong, just potential, I was both floored and afraid. I'd always felt like there was a right and wrong way for me to go before this. I felt an immense sense of responsibility. Like I was leaving home for the first time and had to take care of myself, even though I'd been doing that for a while in many ways.

To be honest, my mind was blown. A philosophy which had once guided me now felt like a lie. Or maybe just one of the steps on the journey of discovery.

I kept thinking back to that moonlit night in County Mayo. No matter what happened, everything would be alright, the moon had said. And I believed her.

It's funny looking back. Everything that happened in Ireland, all the people I met and fell in love with, all the places I discovered and connected to, the new kind of belonging I found there, and the out of placeness I felt being from a different culture and upbringing – it was all just *potential* back then. It was unwritten.

But now, it is. Now it's written. It's this book you're holding in your hands. Or reading through the glow of your screen.

When I finally did decide to move to Ireland, I did it wholeheartedly. And that comforted me in times of struggle and inspired me in times of joy. I chose the journey. It was mine. And I am so grateful for that.

People in this world like to pretend they have all the answers. Not everyone. But a lot of people. It happens in religions. In politics. In relationships. It's a human condition. The need to know. To be certain. To be safe. And I love that!

But I do sense that the vast complexity of the human soul is better expressed through our own deep desires, what we are drawn to and following the quiet voice inside that leads us to places where we *really* thrive. And if we could combine that with community?

I feel like we'd have a much healthier society. Less focused on power struggles, and more focused on creation, co-creation and true safety in our belonging.

Anyway, I digress. But I want to leave you with something.

Once I'd made the move overseas, at one stage I was between houses and living with my friend Jean. I found house hunting to be more challenging than when I'd first moved there. I went to see *all* kinds of places, from large new builds in Glengarriff to musty farmhouses with questionable cleanliness. I really couldn't find the right fit and was starting to struggle. People kept telling me it would all work out, but each time someone said that it just pissed me off. What were they, a fucking hippie? I wanted to shout, "Well are you going to take me in if I can't find anything? Because I promised my friend I'd move out in the next week, and I still haven't found anything suitable."

One day I was sitting with my friend's father. I really liked him. I always felt so calm around him. He had the best eyes – deep, like a well. I told him about my challenge, and he looked at me and said, "Kat, all will be well. You'll find something."

And when he said that I completely relaxed. It was a grounding moment. I knew he was right. My friend's father and the moon were right. All will be well. No matter what, everything will be okay.

A week later I found a place. Funnily enough, it was the friend that I mentioned above who connected me with a woman he knew. She had a beautiful stone cottage on her property and the moment I walked in, I knew the answer for me was yes.

And all was well in my beautiful nowhere. After all, nowhere is still somewhere. Or everywhere, depending on how you look at it.

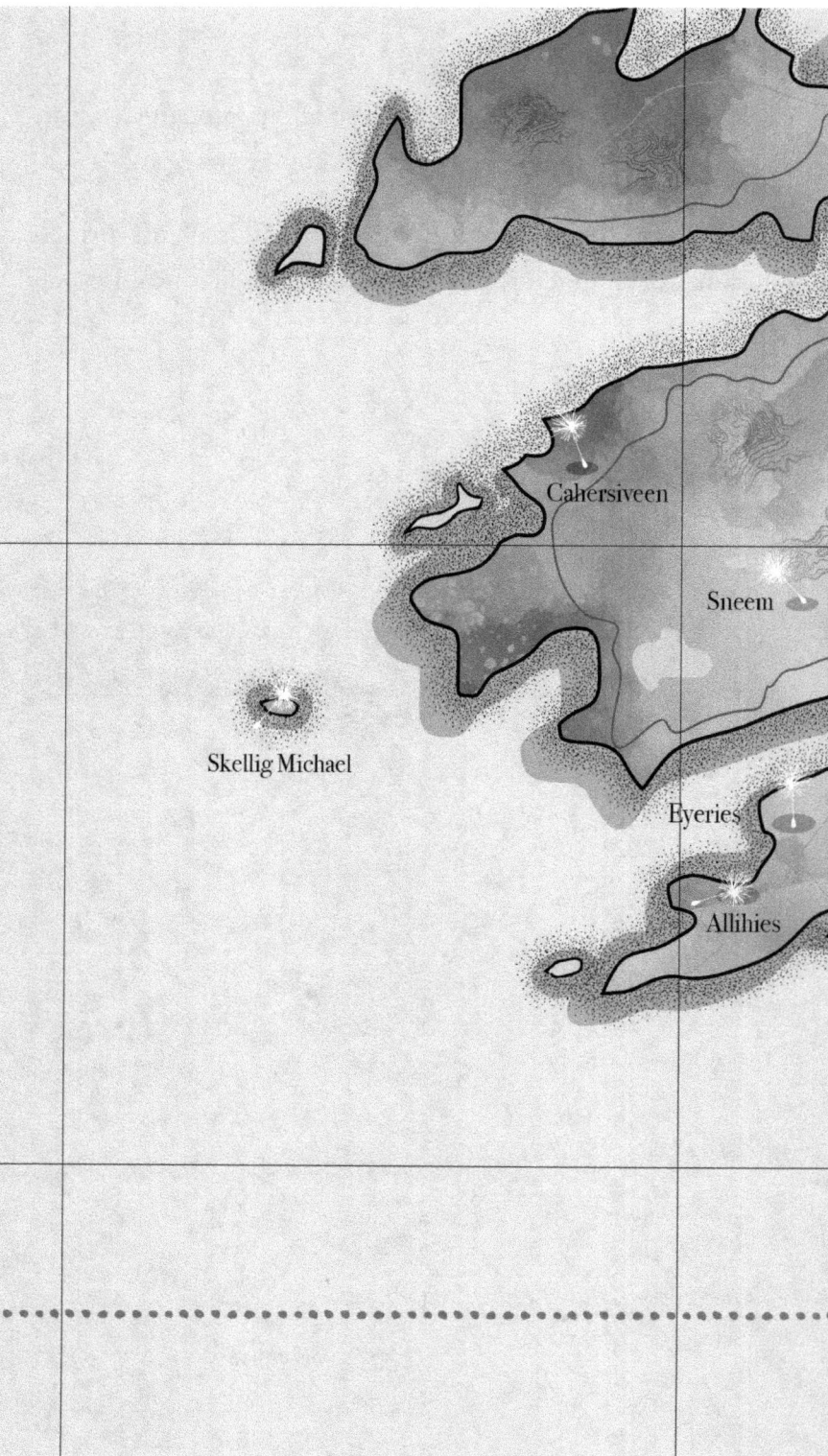

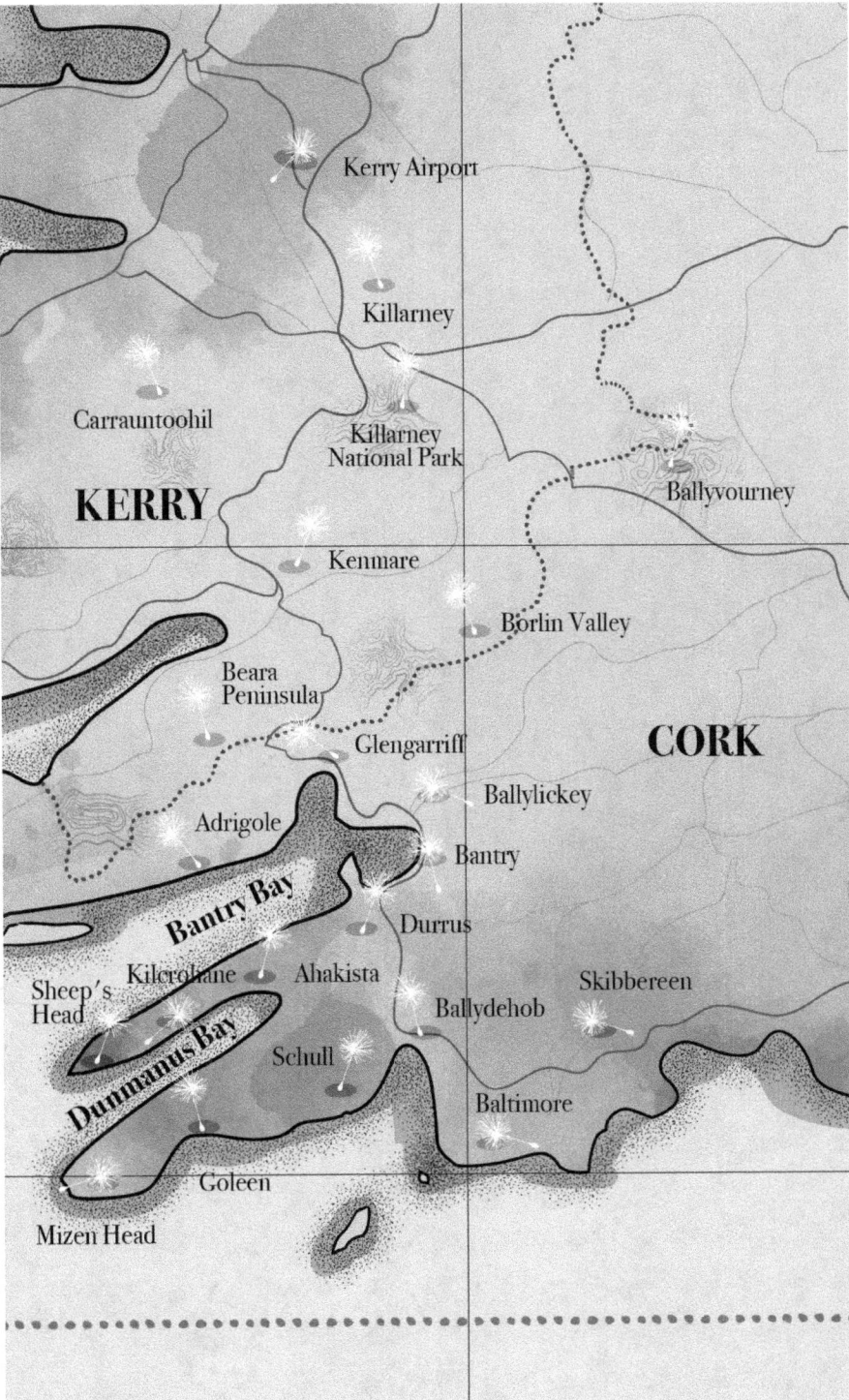

Introduction

"Once we believe in ourselves, we can risk curiosity, wonder, spontaneous delight, or any experience that reveals the human spirit."

-E.E. Cummings

Grab a cup of tea, coffee, or perhaps a glass of wine and enjoy the journey. Welcome to Rainbow Weather!

What is Rainbow Weather?

I magine with me now – it's a wild, spring day in Ireland and we're walking along the coast.

It's partly cloudy. The sun keeps peeking out from behind white, puffy cumulus clouds. To the West, we notice shadowy greys filling the sky which creates this beautiful contrast of both dark and light. Then, rain begins to fall. But the sun? It doesn't disappear. It shines brightly, regardless.

This is rainbow weather.

I lived in West Cork for almost five years, and I'd say I saw at least one rainbow weekly if not more. I started to get a sense of when they would appear after a couple of years of living in the countryside. I'd walk outdoors and see the dark and the light in the sky, rain not yet here, but threatening, sun shining – and I'd get that feeling. I think it might be similar to what some people experience before a snow. Or a tornado. Your senses pick up. You feel it.

And I'd say, "It's rainbow weather" with a big smile on my face, my body vibrating with child-like excitement as I scanned the sky.

Rainbows are a natural phenomenon that occur during mixed weather states. At a very basic level, they are refracted light. Light scattered by raindrops.

Refraction occurs when sunlight changes direction while passing through a medium thicker than air, like a raindrop. Once the light enters a drop, it is reflected off the back and then refracted again as it leaves and travels to our eyes.

Want to know something else kind of crazy about rainbows? Each one is unique to its observer. According to the Royal Meteorological Society in South Africa, "Sunlight is made of many different wavelengths, or colours, that travel at different speeds when passing through a medium."

They continue to say, "This causes the white light to split into different colours. Longer wavelengths appear as red and shorter wavelengths appear as blue or violet. This is not a true spectrum as the colours mix and blur throughout the spectacle. The angle of scatter from raindrops is different for everyone which means that every rainbow is unique to the observer."

I've also come to know rainbow weather as an emotional state. I'm not entirely sure I experienced this fully until I lived in Ireland. It occurs when you are truly sad, tears streaming down your face and then something about the situation or the moment or a memory comes in and makes you laugh and suddenly you are laughing and crying at the same time.

It's funny. There's something relieving about experiencing those emotions together. It feels like they belong, like a pair. And by feeling them together, I'm actually expanding as a human being.

I remember one of the first times I met my friend Pontus. I told him that I kinda had this thing for rainbows and a long-standing question about them.

"If I was standing in a rainbow, would I see it? Or if you were watching me, would you see me in it?"

Pontus had no idea, but he did know where the hose was. It was a sunny day in West Kerry and we attempted to make a rainbow we could step into. While we were unsuccessful, there was a lot of laughter.

One day another friend, Rossa, who you'll hear more about later in this book, sent me a voice note about a rainbow that he was seeing as he drove. He didn't know I had a thing for rainbows, so the fact that he mentioned them made me pay attention. He said that as he drove there was this rainbow right in front of him, moving as he moved. Always just out of reach of the front bumper of his big jeep. Rainbow chaser!

The Maasai people in Kenya see the rainbow as a bad omen. Many Hawaiians believe that when you see a rainbow you are in the right place at the right time. And in Japan, there is a myth or belief that the rainbow is a Floating Bridge of Heaven. Male and female creators of the world descend on this bridge to create land from the ocean of chaos.

I've come to see rainbows as a sign that a big learning opportunity is on the horizon. For me, they have often been connected to people and places that bring up complex emotions. And illusions. And when I sort through all the pieces, open myself up, and step beyond the rainbow, I recognise this – that we are all very, very human. And those complexities make for such amazing moments of beauty. And somehow, it's all just a part of the journey of life, of growth, of change, and of love.

That is where the title of my book stems from. Rainbow Weather is a series of short stories about my five years living in West Cork, along the coast of the Wild Atlantic Way. Each section has a different theme, from the human connections I made to the landscapes I fell in love with, from the work I engaged in, to the guys I dated, and so much more. I chose the short story format because there were so many punctuated moments during my time there, like bright sparks in the mist. So short stories made the most sense to my mind and heart.

They can be read individually, but as you go, you'll begin to see and sense their interconnectedness. The book ends with a special section called Kaleidoscope which contains travel tips, poetry, music, and other pieces of inspiration from my time abroad.

A big portion of the writing of these stories occurred in South Africa, which, strangely enough, is known as the Rainbow Nation. Coined by Archbishop Desmond Tutu after the country's first democratic election, it was meant to describe the coming together of many cultural, racial, and ethnic groups into a unified field. And while this term has recently received interesting and poignant backlash, it strikes me as fitting that I wrote a large portion of my book in this place.

So, what happens these days when I see a rainbow? I take a moment. I pause and notice. And I send out some appreciation. Sometimes I shift my direction internally because I've learned that rainbows appear to help guide me and if I don't listen I will almost 100% end up in some trouble. But sometimes I take the Hawaiian approach, breathe, and know I am exactly where I need to be.

Dandelion Seeds

"Then ask yourself and yourself alone this one question. Does this path have heart? All paths are the same. They lead nowhere. They are paths going through the brush or into the brush or under the brush of the Universe. The only question is: Does this path have heart? If it does, then it is a good path. If it doesn't, then it is of no use."

-Carlos Castaneda

There are pivotal moments that draw all travellers forward towards something intangible – a feeling, a sense or sometimes even a pull. The stories in this section are those kinds of moments and are what put my feet on the road towards Ireland.

1

The Draw of Ireland

Vernon Bellecourt is partially responsible for getting me to Ireland.

Vernon was a member of the Crane Clan of the Anishinaabe Ojibwe. No Irish connections that I know of. Yet the words he spoke to me, to all of us that day back in the year 2000, have always stayed with me.

My boyfriend at the time and I went to see Winona LaDuke speak at Ohio State University. She was Ralph Nader's running mate for the US Presidency on the Green Party ticket, and we were big fans. We walked into the auditorium and were met with a surprise. Her relative, Vernon, was there, getting ready to speak in her stead. She'd had a death in the family and couldn't make the event.

Honestly, I can't remember everything Vernon spoke about that night. I remember he had ... presence. And was slightly intimidating. Kind of like a stern Uncle who you know has wisdom and your best interest at heart, but isn't going to sugar coat anything.

One thing I definitely remember? He took his eyes off the podium, looked up at all of us in the auditorium and said, "*You people need to get in touch with your ancestors.*"

I didn't know why at the time, but those words, they blew in like a cold wind and got into my bones.

I can remember, as a young one, being curious about where my ancestors came from. I'd ask my mom and she'd say things like France and Germany. But when she mentioned Ireland? Something stirred in my five-year-old soul. My bowl cut shimmying with the earnest shake of my head, I told her that one day I was going to go there.

Years later I started studying and then teaching at a place called Wilderness Awareness School, a non-profit dedicated to helping children and adults cultivate healthy relationships with nature, community, and self. While there I had the great privilege to meet and learn from Jake Swamp, a peacemaker from the Wolf Clan of the Mohawk Nation. He shared traditional teachings with Wilderness Awareness School, specifically the Thanksgiving Address, something his people did before any important gathering. It's like a prayer where every aspect of the natural world is acknowledged and given thanks to.

There was one part of the address that I always struggled with when I spoke it, both aloud at our own gatherings and when I was by myself – the part where you thank the ancestors. My mind understood it, the connections that spider web back in time drawing different families together, passing down DNA, beliefs, stories, and experiences. But I couldn't feel the connection and therefore couldn't express the gratitude.

In 2009 I finally took my first trip to Ireland. I remember sitting on a rock overlooking Dunmanus Bay – it's a body of water along the Sheep's Head Peninsula that leads out into the Atlantic Ocean and eventually to Newfoundland. Over the years this spot would become very special to me.

So, sitting on this rock overlooking this bay I spoke the Thanksgiving Address aloud, to the gulls and waves and checkered landscape of West Cork. And do you know what? When I got to the part about my ancestors, I felt something. I felt something! I felt a connection. That's the best way I can describe it. Like a resonance when you sing, and the vibrations fill your body.

And there, I began to very slowly understand Vernon's words from that day, 9 years ago. I sometimes wonder, is this what he meant? That knowing and sensing the lineage where I've come from helps me understand who I am. It doesn't define me. But it's an anchor of honour between myself and all that has come before. Whether I like it or not.

My ancestors lived. They experienced life, learned lessons, held beliefs, created and destroyed, and passed much of that knowledge down to me in the form of spiralling double helixes in my cells. I began to wonder – would calling on them for support, guidance, and understanding, as Jake's tribe does, help me live a more connected and authentic life?

2

Synchronicities, Dreams and Where the Dandelion Seeds Came From

I was sitting under a Western Red Cedar tree when I decided to go to Ireland for the first time.

It was a sunny Sunday afternoon in the Pacific Northwest, and I'd just finished watching a movie called *The Secret of Roan Inish* – a story about a young girl who goes to live with her grandparents on an island off the coast of Ireland when her little brother goes missing at home. The traditional Irish music throughout the film brought me to unexplainable tears and I felt my heart opening. Sitting under that cedar, the sweet smell of her fronds all around me, I had that knowing feeling. I was going to Ireland.

The next day I opened a savings account at my local credit union and so began the slow and steady progress of squirrelling money away for this big dream I had. It was 2007.

In the Fall of 2008, I bought my ticket. That's when I met Ciara. She was dating a friend of mine and had flown over from Ireland to the States for a visit. God, she was funny. In a strip mall Irish pub called JJ Mahoney's, a few doors up from the movie theatre and a few doors down from an Urgent Care, a group of us drank, talked, and peed ourselves with laughter long into the night.

When she found out I was visiting Ireland in the spring she graciously offered to pick me up at the airport and spend some time showing me around her country! From this moment on I noticed a snowball effect of synchronicities and offers that began to shape my trip to Ireland.

I was over the moon about my upcoming travels. I think thrilled would be the most accurate word. So, naturally, I told almost everyone I met, like Ciara, all about it. And you know what I discovered? Two things.

One, people love Ireland! It seemed almost everyone had a story; about one of their own trips or the time one of their friends went or a dream of their hopes to go. It's funny – Ireland became this connecting force, drawing out genuine conversation and excitement. Now, having lived there, I can 100% vouch that Ireland is that kind of place.

Two, I got loads of recommendations for my travels! *"Oh, you've got to go here."* Or *"You've got to meet this person, here's their email address and phone number – don't worry if they don't get back to you, Irish people are terrible at making plans ahead of time, but when you arrive, reach out again."*

I told my friend John about my trip, and he burst into a happy walk down memory lane about his time with this guy up in Connemara. Then he gave me his email address and told me I should get in touch with him and go for a visit. The man seemed incredible – a community organiser, storyteller, and school principal!

I told my friend Maeve about my trip and suddenly I was set to go and stay with her mom outside Galway.

This kind of thing kept happening. I got invites, travel suggestions, and general goodwill over and over and over again to the point that I was certain something out of the ordinary was happening. Magic was definitely afoot. And it built up this momentum for my trip. Like a slip 'n slide into the country.

And then, about one month before my April 15th, 2009 departure date, something happened.

Have you ever been touched deeply by a dream? I awoke early one spring morning, still in Washington, to fresh snow and a telephone call that work was cancelled. Snow was rare where I lived, winters being filled with rain and mist instead of ice and cold. As I hung up, the sun streamed in through my big bedroom windows illuminating everything inside the house and brightening the white of the snow on the balcony. It felt so good to bask in that sunshine.

I lay there daydreaming and then I was asleep – the transition back to dreaming completely seamless.

I was high up, in a very tall building. The land around me was a patchwork – greens and browns separated by stonewalls. And in the distance was the ocean, lightly misted over.

I remember the sky – oh that sky! It was the most vivid cornflower blue I've ever seen. And all around me, floating, were dandelion seed heads, suspended in colour.

I don't know how long I stayed there immersed in this place, but it felt timeless. When I awoke the transition was seamless once again. I slid from cornflower blue to warm sunshine to snow. My eyes opened. I'm usually jolted out of dreams or have trouble remembering them at first. I felt indescribably happy. This dream felt like a gift.

I find some things in life are best described, experienced, and integrated through the arts, like poetry, music, or painting. I like to let logic sit beside me as I take in what feels like these 'knowings' that seem to appear when I'm open.

After this most delicious and vivid dream, I had one of these knowings – that Ireland was one of the homes of my heart.

And all of this pre-trip synchronicity and good cheer? This was Ireland's foreplay. When my feet touched Irish soil for the first time these magic moments continued – like a string of pearls, each unique, connected, and flowing one to the next. And because of this, I began to trust in the flow of life in a way I'd never done before.

My life would never be the same.

3

Sheila and the Wedding

I t was getting late, and I found myself slow dancing with a Scottish woman called Elaine.

Elaine was the organiser of the swing dancing night I was attending in this little pub in Cork City. I hadn't moved to Ireland yet, mind you. No, I was on one of my many exploratory trips. I didn't know very many people there, but it didn't matter. The thing about Ireland? You're never really alone.

As Elaine and I slow danced, conversation trickled in between spins, and I mentioned I was headed down to the Sheep's Head Peninsula to visit a friend. She paused for a moment in her swaying, a look of surprise on her face, and then told me, unequivocally, that I needed to meet Sheila Ellis. Sheila, she told me, was a swing dancer, a carpenter, a teacher, and a hostess with the mostess. Elaine also just happened to be her best friend.

She gave me Sheila's number and told me to get in touch with her when I got down there. I saved the number in my phone and for whatever reason never called Miss Ellis.

Fast forward now two years later. I was in Cork City on another Ireland exploration. I found myself at the same swing dance in the same bar and once again in the arms of Elaine, the swing dancer. She followed up with me.

"Did you meet Sheila?" she asked excitedly.

When I said no, Elaine was on it again. She told me that she was going down to see Sheila on the Sheep's Head for a party the coming weekend and that I should meet up with them! I was already planning on going down there to visit my friend Jean, so I said yes, of course, I'd call by the party. And then we left it! No details or directions, nothing. For some reason that didn't bother my American soul. I had their numbers. This was Ireland. It was going to work out.

When I walked in the door of Jean's green cottage a few days later, Blotto, her handsome black lab greeted me with a wag and a nuzzle. We embraced and then I excitedly told her about this party.

"Have you heard anything?" I asked, knowing news travels fast in small places.

"Well, not really," she said, "but there was a wedding that happened today, and the couple is having their reception at the Tin Pub?"

To be completely honest I don't know what came over us, but somehow, we decided this might very well be the party Elaine told me about and we drove ourselves down there to investigate.

The first thing I remember when I opened the car door outside of the Tin Pub was the sound of Lynyrd Skynyrd's song Sweet

Home Alabama floating out from the garden behind. My jaw dropped. I wasn't expecting such classic American rock at an Irish wedding. It turns out that the Irish have a big love for American music. I can't tell you how many times I heard Tracy Chapman or Ray Charles passing an Irish singer's lips.

Hand to metal I opened the front door of the pub and walked through to the tent attached out the back. The first person to meet me was the bride. She was beautiful, classically dressed in a form-fitting white gown, a large opaque bow covering her chest. She was also very, very drunk. That didn't stop her from sensing we were crashing her wedding; she knew it right away. But she did something completely unexpected and welcomed us with open arms, telling us to make ourselves at home!

The room was pulsing with Irish people. And through the crowd, I saw Elaine towards the back of the tent. Moments later I met Sheila Ellis, the legend herself. Dressed in a light blue satin pencil skirt dress with a white top and a smile that lit up the room. We'd only started to chat and introduce ourselves, maybe one-minute tops we were speaking when the musicians began playing a swingin' tune with a 1960s kind of vibe. Sheila reached out her hand towards me, the international signal for, do you wanna dance? And out we went, almost strangers, twisting and turning, sweating and laughing across the dance floor.

Sheila invited me to visit her the next day for tea. The moment I walked into her home (which was still under construction back then) I had a feeling that this place could be the place I'd been looking for. A dream had begun to take shape in my mind – I wanted to run a yoga retreat in Ireland. I'd done some market research, and no other foreigners were doing that kind of thing, probably because there isn't consistent sun or a tropical vibe. But I wasn't planning on a traditional-style yoga retreat. I wanted to incorporate nature and culture right alongside yoga, making it more of an adventure retreat with an emphasis on relaxation and transformation.

Her unfinished home sat at a high point on the hill overlooking Dunmanus Bay. She had a large rectangular room right in the front of the house with two sets of double doors that opened up to the view. The upstairs was going to have two bedrooms. That, combined with the other two next door in the already completed, semi-attached cottage, made it feasible to hold a retreat! It felt like this place was the right combination of cosy, unique, and functional for my small bespoke dreams. I was floored.

As we sipped our tea Sheila told me the story of her home. The original cottage was a dwelling house that had once been used as a cow, turkey, and spud storage shed, now entirely refurbished into a snug home complete with one of those traditionally large Irish fireplaces. The extension had been in the making for years, both she and volunteers working on it when she had time off from her full-time job as a carpentry teacher at a private school in Bandon. This woman was so impressive – a creative and an artisan, my favourite combination.

Two years later Sheila Ellis and I partnered together and ran my first-ever Retreat to Ireland. We had 3 participants. It was magic. We went to the Ballydehob Jazz Festival, hiked to the old copper miner's stone houses far out on the Sheep's Head and saved a stuck lamb in the process. We did yoga every morning in Sheila's front room, visited a lot of pubs and even tried our hand at céili dancing a couple of times!

Sometimes I think about meetings like these. Elaine, myself, and Sheila. How a series of spider web-like experiences actually lead to something! The kind of something that has an element of magic, fate or synchronicity.

It feels like all of these moments of meeting are like open door-ways, with a chance to walk through, or not. What if I'd never met Elaine? What if I'd never mentioned the Sheep's Head? What if Elaine hadn't followed up with me about Sheila the 2nd time we met and urged me to meet up with them? How would my life have changed? Would I have met Sheila anyway?

These are the kinds of questions that fill me with curiosity and wonder, like looking at a clear night sky or waking up from a potent dream. And the ease with which these kinds of connections are made belong to Ireland like no other place I've travelled to. I have absolutely no idea how it works, I simply know that it does. I've lived it. Over and again.

4

Sheila and the Standing Stone

There is something so beautiful and mysterious about Standing Stones, don't you think?

Always a story to be discovered and some peace to be found. But I didn't realise how magic they could be until one beautiful afternoon after my second Retreat to Ireland when my friend Sheila and I went for a mini adventure. We *loved* mini adventures. Our aim? Get in the car and follow our intuition until we found something cool. Little did we know the strange series of events that would soon unfold...

"Whoa, look at that stone!" Sheila exclaimed as we rounded a bend on one of the many twisting back roads of West Cork. And her exclamation was on point! There, sitting on a hill, stood both a tall and very wide standing stone, illuminated by the setting sun. As our car crept along like a stalker, I began to wonder, how did that stone come to be in that field out in the middle of nowhere?

Casually, as if reading my mind, Sheila said, "Let's go ask the farmer about it." And because I so wanted to and Sheila was a local, I thought, why not? "Yes, let's!"

We drove up the dirt-tracked driveway and into a small cattle yard just in time to see the farmer and some 15 cows come in from the fields beyond. Good timing.

After a friendly, but somewhat suspicious greeting from the farmer upon our unexpected arrival, he asked us to wait while he finished up with the cows. Our tennis shoes wandered around the mucky dirt as we waited. I spotted a few horseshoes up on the wall of his barn. It's a tradition here in Ireland to place horseshoes with the opening facing up, like a U, to catch good luck and abundance.

When the last cow was secured, just as promised, our mysterious farmer came towards us and began a conversation that blew (and still does blow) my mind.

First, it turns out the standing stone was a mystery, even to experts. The University of Cork had been out to investigate – they measured its dimensions, mapped its location, and added it to their data of the many Neolithic monuments of the area. But no conclusion as to what it was used for or who brought it there had been made. As our conversation wound through many topics, including this beautiful mystery of a stone, it was discovered that the farmer, Martin, grew up in Ahakista. That's where Sheila grew up too! Turns out Sheila was good friends with one of Martin's sisters called Caroline. It's always a lovely (and relieving moment for many Irish people) when you can place your connections to one another.

This whole experience was just so magical for me that, in the privacy of my own mind I thought ... wouldn't it be amazing if I too was somehow connected to this man?

The likelihood seemed slim, the conversation continued, and the sun slowly began to make its way down toward the horizon. Martin spoke more about the stone, about his farm, and then about his other siblings. When he mentioned a sister that lived in the US and ran retreats in Durrus, my ears perked up.

To this day, I remember the sensation of that moment. It was as if a rusty cog in my brain slowly, painfully, began to turn, trying to dig up a memory, or something, related to what Martin was saying. Luckily this cog continued its circular movements, and I had the clarity to pull out my phone. The battery was at 2%. I struggled to open Facebook, pulling from the one bar of reception I was getting and finally managed to find what I was looking for. A Facebook profile of one of my friends.

"Is this your sister?" I asked,

"Why, yes, it is!" Martin said.

My phone died and Sheila and I both screamed with excitement. It turns out that this woman, Marion, and Martin's other sister, had contacted me ages ago. She somehow found my Retreat to Ireland website and got in touch saying she was doing retreats on the Sheep's Head too and that we should connect. And so, we became Facebook friends but had never met in person. Yet here I was, speaking with her brother, the guardian of the standing stone!

Sheila and I were buzzing. We headed back to the farmyard and in my excitement, I asked Martin if, by any chance, I could have one of his horseshoes. The experience of meeting him and all the synchronicities felt so beautiful and lucky that I wanted something to remember it all by. I'd been looking for a horseshoe to add to my own home back in the States for the last couple of weeks, but had been waiting for just the right fit. And bless that man, he gave me one. I have it to this day.

But the adventure didn't end there...

We headed into Bantry town to get a bite to eat. The sun had almost completely set by now and we were ravenous. We stepped into Wharton's, a brightly lit fish & chips shop and hungrily ate our cod and chips and mushy peas, musing over our adventure. What a day!

Then we stepped back into the night, intending to get in the car and head home. But life had other plans. We ran into an acquaintance of Sheila's who was with his friend. They were heading into Ma Murphy's for a pint and invited us along. This was the beginning of a friendship for me, but I had no idea at the time. The man who was with Sheila's friend was called Cian. And because of another few magic encounters with him (which I'll save for another story), Cian became one of my closest friends for a while in Ireland.

The next day, Sheila got a text from Caroline. Remember Caroline? The sister Sheila knew through Martin the Farmer? Caroline messaged knowing nothing of what had happened the day before.

She said that she was in a taxi at the Dublin airport and got to chatting with the cabby. He asked her where she was from and when she said Ahakista on the Sheep's Head, he paused.

"Funny," he said, "I had a woman in here right before you. She was from Seattle and was just down in Ahakista at a yoga retreat."

Sheila and I screamed for the second time in the last 24 hours. Retreat to Ireland 2014 had just ended and we knew it was one of our participants!

Sheila busied herself with texting Caroline back to give her the full story of magic that had unfolded in the last day. And I let my mind float back to the standing stone in Martin's field.

Incorporated into a stone wall with a little hawthorn tree planted beside it, its sheer size still blowing my mind, the memory of the sun illuminating it as it set. Back then (and even now I'd say), Ireland seemed a truly magic place, where the veil between your own thoughts and reality was thin and events that seemed only to belong in whimsical novels took place in real life. Standing Stone, Martin, Caroline, Marion, Cian ... they all became connected that fine summer's day.

This experience built more momentum in my mind and heart toward moving to Ireland. I wanted to experience more magic like this.

5

The Old Filing Cabinet

It was autumn in Ohio and I was home visiting my mom. I was also aching for Ireland.

All around me, the leaves had begun to change; greens mixing with reds, yellows, oranges, golds ... death and sugar and so much beauty.

I was dreaming of returning to Ireland. In fact, I'd been dreaming of it since the moment I left the country after my first trip in in May 2009. Months had passed and I was searching for a way to spend a longer stretch of time there. My research so far had revealed that Ireland and the US didn't have a great working visa arrangement for someone like me. So my mind wandered and twisted and turned. Until I remembered something – my dad was born in Canada! This thought felt like bright hope in the darkness, so I brought my fingers to the keyboard once more to research.

Turns out, the options were much better for getting a working holiday visa as a Canadian. I picked up the phone and contacted the Canadian Embassy to tell them about my situation. My dad was born in Canada in 1943 and was adopted by Americans in 1949. It turns out that Canada had updated legislation to allow adopted children to reclaim their citizenship and because of that I would have a claim. I was floored.

I reached out to my dad after this discovery to begin the process of collecting all the official documents I needed for the application. Unfortunately, he never responded. This didn't surprise me. He wasn't in my life in any real way and hadn't made an effort over the years. My bright hope of returning to Ireland took pause again. The leaves continued to fall. I continued to dream.

I don't know why, but I kept noticing this tall, metal filing cabinet in my mom's basement each time I'd go downstairs. It had been there since my childhood. Four deep metal drawers, tall, grey, cold, and always a bit of a mystery. One day I asked my mom about it. What was in that thing?

Turns out the filing cabinet held papers belonging to my dad and his business. My mom had kept them all these years, afraid to throw them away. You see, when he left her, not long before their divorce, the IRS showed up at her door. Apparently, my father owed a big sum of back taxes. My mom's name was on a lot of his business documents back then. She did it to help him because, as the story goes, he had trouble with his adoption and citizenship paperwork and needed a co-signer to make his business valid. And because of this, she was legally liable even though she had no real part in the running or maintenance of his affairs. Yikes.

Thanks to a good lawyer and a law about spousal ignorance, my mom didn't end up having to pay. But she was scarred by the experience and had decided to keep the filing cabinet, just in case.

After looking up the limit on tax fraud and determining she was well beyond it, we decided to clear that baby out and send all those documents to the shredder!

The drawers stuck a little as we tried to pull them open, the roller wheels inching along their tracks. Paper by paper we pulled each item out and took a look. Hours went by. My mom called the mobile shredder. We laughed. I could sense her relief as we brought this painful chapter to a new form of closed.

And wouldn't you know it? In the bottom drawer of that dusty old thing, we found every single piece of documentation I needed to get my Canadian citizenship – my dad's adoption papers, his original passport, letters between the adoption agency and the people who would become my grandparents. Every single piece was there. It was a little miracle.

I completed all my paperwork and filed it at the embassy. I received one confirmation letter that explicitly stated not to reach out for more information, and that the government would be in touch when they were ready. Nine months later I received my citizenship card. I was a Canadian!

It would be about four years before I'd take advantage of the working holiday visa available between Ireland and Canada and move abroad. But the moment that slim letter from Canada arrived in my metal post office box, a whole new world of possibilities opened up.

Who do you Belong To?

"Drifting off to sleep, I thought about her. How nobody is perfect. How you just have to close your eyes and breathe out and let the puzzle of the human heart be what it is."

-Sue Monk Kidd

I was once picked up hitchhiking by an elderly gentleman in Bandon, a small town in West Cork. Bandon is famous for being the birthplace of Graham Norton, that, and some epic floods. After our initial greeting and the formality of making sure we were going the same way, I jumped in the car. There was a moment of silence and then he said, "So, who do you belong to?" in a thick, country accent, clothed in wool, a farmer by all accounts. This is part of the colloquial poetry of Ireland and a way to ask, who are your relations?

While the stories here in no way detail any blood relatives, they do share about the people I belonged to, who touched my life, both briefly and long term.

To all the beautiful people I spent time with in Ireland – this is for you.

6

I Know I Know You

My first job in Ireland was waiting tables and making coffee for this great little café called Manning's Emporium in the townland of Ballylickey.

You could see Bantry Bay from the colourful barrel tables we rolled out each morning. Inside was a small, specialty goods grocery store and deli where customers could purchase locally produced meats and cheeses and order from a simple menu that varied seasonally.

Manning's was started in 1946. Mr. and Mrs. Manning reared Jersey cows on nearby pastures and supplied local hotels and restaurants with milk, cream, and butter. Soon, locals began asking for butter for themselves, and Manning's was born! The business continued to develop over the years and was taken over by their son Val in the 1970s, just as the West Cork food scene was gaining an international reputation. Manning's became synonymous with quality and attracted customers from near and far who came looking specifically for local and international offerings.

It's a truly unique little spot with great coffee! I discovered it by accident on my travels in Ireland before ever moving over. I was researching a remote valley I'd become enamoured with.

A friend of mine had driven me through it on our way from Kenmare to Bantry and I wanted to know everything about it. I ended up finding a cycling forum that mentioned the Valley and Manning's. Apparently, the coffee was so good, the cyclists liked to extend one of their routes to include a stop at the café.

Anyway, one busy spring day I was sweating and dancing between tables doing my waitress thing when a lovely woman came up to me.

"I know I know you," she said.

Sounds kinda creepy when I write it now, but in the moment it just wasn't. It was obvious she thought she recognised me but couldn't place how in her mind.

We chatted for a while trying to figure it out. I didn't recognise her at all. Not a speck. And none of my prompts were helping her memory.

"*It'll come to me,*" she said and went to sit back down at her table.

Well, it was so busy I plumb forgot about her and continued clearing tables, getting people cappuccinos, and forgetting my own name let alone how she knew she knew me.

45 minutes later this woman, Maeve was her name, reappeared.

"I know how I know you!" she exclaimed with bright eyes and a little bit of mischief in her smile.

"My husband and I saw you sing a song at Matt Molloy's pub up in Westport."

Now I want you to understand something. Westport is in County Mayo. We were down in County Cork, some 205 miles south. Irish roads are *small* so that's a driving time of over 4 ½ hours. It's far for Irish standards.

For the first time, I understood the Irish word gobsmacked. It means utterly astonished or astounded according to Merriam Webster.

In the summer of 2014, about six months before I ended up moving to Ireland, I was travelling, exploring, and running a retreat. My mom joined me for part of the time and we'd gone up the country to County Mayo. We were both really curious about the 14th-century pirate queen, Grania O'Malley, and her former stronghold was up in Mayo.

One night we ventured into Westport, specifically to check out Matt Molloy's pub. Matt was the flute player in the famous Irish band The Chieftains and his pub was renowned for its amazing music sessions.

When my mom and I wandered in, the pub was packed! Luckily an Irish couple took pity on us and brought us to sit at their table. They were great craic. It was hard to hear each other over the six or seven musicians playing in the session, but eventually, the couple found out I was a singer. 15 minutes later I was called up to sing for the crowd. I'll never forget it. I was so surprised! The man of the couple snuck up and told the band that an American singer was there!

And that is where Maeve, the woman who said I know I know you, first knew me. She and her husband had been there that night, and they'd heard me sing. She said I had a beautiful voice. I took a photo of us in Manning's Emporium that day so I would always remember this magic moment that brought us together.

It's funny. The day after the night I sang in Matt Molloy's I climbed Croagh Patrick, one of Ireland's holiest mountains. Once on the way up and once on the way down I had someone stop me to say they'd been at the pub that night too and loved my voice. Little did I know that months and months later I would experience the exact same thing in a completely different place. I mean come on ... what are the chances?

7

Pat and the Hilltop

When I first moved to Ireland in 2015, I felt as if I'd left the mainstream current of the world and entered a side pool of slow-moving, amber water.

I used to drive little back roads and explore using my senses and intuition. Sometimes a feeling would pull me one way or a little sign saying something mysterious like *Maulingard* would take me another.

And you know what? I loved it. I was so used to schedules and linear lines and being (what I then considered) responsible, that this newfound sense of freedom felt like swimming in the pool they describe at the end of the book *The Neverending Story*. Warm. Full of joy. Bubbling.

One afternoon I drove up a tiny road to a little hilltop I'd discovered overlooking Dunmanus Bay to sit and play guitar. Blue holes appeared between white, fluffy clouds and the breeze was doing her thing as Gregory Alan Isakov and old folk songs passed my lips, disappearing into the atmosphere.

I was searching for some peace and privacy that day, but Ireland, as she does, had other plans for me. In the distance, climbing up the tiny road to my perch was a red Mustang!

His name was Pat. He was out for a drive with his friend, an Asian woman in grad school for something I cannot remember. But I do remember that Pat got out of his car and just stood and listened to me play before a word passed his lips. And for some reason, I kept playing, like I was gigging at a pub, and the music must go on.

We talked on that rock for over an hour, having a conversation that can only be described as perfectly winding; something unique to the moment we found ourselves in made up of the kind of openness, friendship, and respect that is easily shared between strangers. It's something that happens quite often in Ireland, and I believe it's something that happens quite often to people who are enjoying the moment while they travel.

The Irish are great conversationalists and it's easy to go back and forth on all sorts of topics without ever batting an eyelash. That hour felt like nothing as the sun came and went and the breeze kept up with her movements. I remember feeling that something unique was happening. I remember feeling totally open to the connection. And I remember feeling alive and grateful. Sometimes it's the little moments that make for rich memories.

Before they went on their way Pat took photos of us together on the hilltop and got my email address. Some days later I received two emails with photos from our time together, the first of which had this subject line: You are a very special person.

Years later I'd discover that Pat was an art lover. He would visit Annabel Langrish's gallery on the Sheep's Head Peninsula frequently and especially on sunny days to check out her new pieces and have lunch in the garden. I'm guessing Pat loved that hilltop too. At the very pinnacle, you can see both Dunmanus and Bantry Bays, a surround sound of landscape and ocean beauty. It is a very special place. I suppose that's why we met there.

8

A Quick Eternity

The moment he touched my hand I was lifted.

Like bubbles filled up the inside of my body, surrounding me at the same time. I felt waves of warmth when we shook hands. Like his touch magnified the happiness already inside me. How could a handshake do that?

"I'm Con," he said, Irish eyes sparkling.

I smiled. "Kat," I replied, putting my hand to my heart.

Work was so busy. There was a long line of people crowded into an already tiny café, and even more were spilling out the doors and into the parking lot. It was hectic! Everyone behind the counter had twisted looks of stress on their faces and the vibe was just short of strained.

But me? I was weaving! With a bright smile on my face, I bussed tables and gave information and took orders. I wanted to lift the vibe up and make it fun. Because none of us needed the experience to be so tense, no matter how crammed we were into a small space wanting our food, coffee, or wine!

Then Con stopped me with his bubbles and his sparkles, and the moment slowed down and then became timeless, flowing. And what were only 30 seconds in a linear context felt stretched and full of nourishment. This is what I like to call a quick eternity.

The first time I ever felt this was with my friend Tim in Washington. I remember he was on his cell phone talking to his sister and I leaned against his left arm at an angle that allowed me to look up. I saw Big Leaf Maple leaves with blue sky and white clouds in between. And there was something about that moment. The conversation. The smell of him. The way my mind drifted in and out of the words he spoke as my heart beat. The moment felt timeless. Like it goes on even now.

I don't experience quick eternities all the time, especially with other people, so when I do, I pay attention. It requires a strong level of receptivity and a quiet mind. It's only requirement? To simply feel. One of the things that Ireland taught me is that feeling is a gift and that sometimes, feelings are meant to be followed. It's part of what makes the culture of Ireland so unpredictable, dare I say disorganised. People follow their feelings. And feelings are such fluid things, moving like the wind, the tide, the river. Changing, always changing.

I ran into Con a few more times over my years in West Cork. But it was the waking dream I had of him after we first met that has stayed with me all these years later. I was walking the road to Barely Lake and he came into my mind. The mist was floating across and in between the surrounding mountains and I had this strange sense that Con was married to the land. That he had given himself to the land of Ireland and was responsible for renewing its magic. Don't ask me to explain how this came to me. It just did. Like an idea, only deeper.

Researching some facts for this story I looked up Con on the internet and found a bio of his. Here is what it says:

"From an early age, Con has been awake to the spirit of this magical place, its shape, and nature combining with its Gaelic culture and spiritual history to weave a rich tapestry of influence. Throughout his life, the intriguing story of Ireland and its people has been a passion for Con, and sharing this with travellers is a privilege he is grateful for."

9

Harvest Moon

I could feel the moon before it ever rose that night. It was almost full, and I knew the moment it appeared over the horizon it would be all big, golden and glowing.

The anticipation tickled me from the inside out – I didn't want to howl, but I was definitely in the mood for magic. And mischief.

Inspired, I decided last minute to meet some friends and drive to Schull for the Harvest Moon Festival. I drove around the sea, over the mountain and into the village. I arrived at one of the participating pubs, pulled open the heavy door and walked right into the celebrations, they were already under way. I moved through the throngs of people packing its funny little maze-like rooms. It was sunset and the light was quickly fading, turning the pub darker. Did I have a drink? I can't remember.

I do remember when we bumped into each other. I'll never forget it. Me, a foot or so below the height of you, our bodies close because of the busyness. And I swear, the world truly and utterly stopped for a moment.

I only felt you and me.

The noise of the room faded, and stillness surrounded us while the outside world kept swirling, like an impressionist painting.

This meeting, it felt intuitive, and instinctual. Like our bodies were talking to each other while our minds witnessed the experience. You smelled so good. And looked so out of place in that place. Like your spirit was calling you elsewhere, but you weren't listening. The world stopped while we talked, like a deep breath. And then we were flung back into the dance.

I have never experienced anything like that before (or since) we met that night. It felt like it belonged only to us and the moment. And to me? It was a green light, even though, as the night progressed, I found myself surrounded with some bright red flags you didn't even know you were holding.

I had to know what it was that I experienced with you in that moment of calm. I had to find out. And I did. Slowly, but surely, we became friends. And it was every bit as complicated as the unfolding of that Harvest Moon night.

One of my favourite memories though, of our complex connection, was the night I saw you blow short puffs of air onto your niece's forehead, teasing her.

When I think back, I'm not sure how it all happened. It was a simple thing really. We were having dinner in Kenmare as we always did. At the end of the evening you, a total gentleman as my friend Jean used to say, walked me out into the cool night air to say goodbye. I had a long drive home and needed to turn around early the next morning and return to Kenmare for work.

You stood beside my green car as I went to turn the old Ford key in the ignition. There was a clog somewhere. My car churned and churned; the starter just wasn't firing right.

"Give it a moment before you start again" you said.

I paused. Took a breath. And then another. Nothing. But you told me to stick with it and eventually, after a good five minutes it finally came to life.

That's when you sprang into action. Ever thoughtful and knowing what I needed sometimes before even I did, you said: "Kat, why don't you stay with me tonight? If your car doesn't start in the morning at least you'll be closer to Kenmare, and we'll figure out how to get you there and back."

I'm pretty sure a sigh escaped my lips. I wasn't used to having men take care of me this way. It felt so good.

"Thank you. I'd love that." I said, my cheeks blushing a little, though the darkness hid it.

As we drove our separate cars back on the long, windy road, across the Caha Pass and down into County Cork you called me on my cell phone to work through some more details. Your voice, deep and Irish with a hint of American, told me if my car wouldn't start in the morning, that you'd take me to work and figure out how to get me home later. As we spoke, I noticed how the fear I sometimes felt around you wasn't there, only a little bit afterward. I'd had such a crush on you it seemed to get in the way of connecting sometimes.

When I ended the call, I could see the moon, quarter-sized in the sky. Only a couple of days ago I realised how long it had been since I'd seen it.

You raced ahead at that funny little bend past the nature reserve in Glengarriff where we'd pretend like we were driving in the USA. And I arrived at the home of you and your parents to find you standing by your van holding a little baby. Your niece. You sent short puffs of air out from your lips, playing with her hair. And her eyes tracked the world – me, you, the dog with his matted fur, me, then back to you again. You held her with love. And there was a closeness there. It was such a beautiful little moment.

You set me up in the conservatory and brought me blankets and a glass of water. You showed me how everything worked and said I could feel free to come into the main house for the bathroom, tea, and snacks, just basically to make myself at home. In my mind I was trying to make myself as inconspicuous as possible; I'll just crash in the conservatory, pee along the fence, and rush out in the morning so I won't disturb anyone. But instead, you made me feel at home. It was no big deal.

I got to see your room too. It was so much bigger than I expected. Tall ceilings. A little sitting area. Clean and spacious. And all your old man sweaters hanging from a clothes rack, like a granddad fashion shoot. We hugged goodnight. I felt contentment.

As I lay on your green leather couch surrounded by plants and round windows and interesting wood, I felt so calm and at ease. I felt taken care of. I guess I felt whole. I think it started on the drive over too. I suddenly felt very down to earth, and all my intuitions about us, possibilities, and fantasies, like a gorgeous rainbow, subsided. I felt the greenness of the coming summer, saw the Glengarriff sign clear as day as I drove (even though it was nearing midnight) and I started to cry. I realised how selfish and caught up I had been in myself, my desires, my needs, my, my, my, that I hadn't even realised you'd truly become my friend.

The green leather on the couch was smooth, but a little sticky on my skin as I sweated. I watched a movie with Whoopie Goldberg and one of the Baldwin brothers. As I started to fall asleep my breathing began to slow. Inhale. And exhale, tracking the sensation as I rested. Breathing and feeling, like I'd learned in all my yoga classes. Breathing and feeling like I still do even now. But this time it was with more ease. The blanket you let me borrow and your friendship kept me safe that night. And I fell asleep, happy, content, and free.

10

It's like Golf with a D

I'll never forget the day I met Dolf.

I was Couchsurfing with a guy my friend called Hugh Grant, simply because she'd misheard his name. Hugh wasn't an actor at all. He was a flautist and sold colourful rugs from overseas locally. But the nickname stuck, and he would forever be known in my memories as such.

Mr. Grant decided to take me to the Bantry Market, a weekly Friday event with stalls full of antiques and clothes, produce and farm animals. It was one of the most unique markets I'd ever been to. One time a guy was selling Magpie traps! Magpies belong to the Family Corvidae, the same one that Ravens and Crows do. They are super smart birds and I'm pretty certain they could outsmart that contraption.

But this time at the market? This was my first time.

We drove along the ocean, the water peaking with a small wind. On our way to Bantry, we stopped in the village of Durrus and entered the post office, a small building on a corner, right next to a pub. Durrus had four or five pubs at the time but the village had a population of 300 people. So many pubs for such a small place!

It was a crossroads of sorts, but I always wondered how that came to be.

It was a sunny day in early May, trees were blossoming, and I was so excited to be out of the house. I'd been in Ireland for over three weeks, relying on the kindness of strangers and my hosts to get where I wanted to go.

Bantry herself, the largest town in the area, is home to about 3,000 people and sits at the mouth of Bantry Bay, one of Ireland's deepest harbours. It stretches 35 kilometres out to the sea and is rich with marine life – things like dolphins, kelp forests and mackerel.

Once we arrived, Hugh decided to take me to the Stuffed Olive – known for its coffee and cakes, he said it was a must-see while in town. As we walked down New Street, I was taking in all the signage; Harrington Estates, The Bake House, SuperValu, and just before the entrance to what is now the old location of the Stuffed Olive, we met Dolf.

"It's like golf with a 'D'," he said. I laughed.

Dolf is a unique human being. Optimistic to a fault, completely genuine, and back in the day he could take a small run and jump up about six feet to land on a concrete post. He has also been known to take long runs in Wellington boots!

Anyway, Dolf found out I was interested in trying céili dancing, so he took my number, told me he'd do a little research, and give me a call.

One week later I got a mysterious voicemail.

By this time, I had moved on to the Beara Peninsula, gardening as a volunteer from 9 am – 2 pm and exploring until sunset. I had to listen to this voice message at least 3 times to decipher what the man was telling me. It was Dolf! He spoke fast and his accent, a mix of Irish and Flemish (his parents were from Belgium), made it hard to understand. I finally figured out that he'd found a dance and was inviting me to attend with him.

And somehow, his invite slotted perfectly into my travel plans. I was headed back to Bantry on the exact night he'd invited me to go dancing. My plan had been to spend the night and catch an early morning bus to Limerick. It felt like fate! So, of course, I said yes.

Dolf picked me up at the grim hostel I had booked for the night in Bantry and drove us on the small backroads to a Gaeltacht village called Ballyvourney. He regaled me with stories and, I kid you not, urged a cow out of the middle of the road as he drove with his hand out of the window using a lot of loud whoops!

We arrived in the village and parked at the Abbey Hotel, entering a back door into what I can only describe as a large room that looked like a community hall. It was filled with people of all ages dancing in the classic circle patterns of céili dancing. And their footwork! It was like tap dancing amid the folk dancing – both men and women adding shuffles and foot rhythms as they swung their partners round and round. Little did I know that the people of Ballyvourney were serious dancers!

Luckily, they welcomed me with open arms, right onto the dance floor. And like a happy fool, I took all my partner-dancing knowledge and did my best to follow along. It was awesome.

I danced with Dolf. And farmers. Women with stern looks on their faces who finally broke into smiles watching my mistakes. And sometimes, when the heat and burning of my calf muscles would become too much for me, I'd sit on the sidelines and watch everyone, a Lady's Guinness in my hand. A Lady's Guinness is a half pint with blackcurrant juice mixed in. It's lovely.

When the night wound down to a close, Dolf and I got back into his red Seat Ibiza and began making our way down the tiny country lanes back to West Cork. We made little stops along the way and talked well into the early morning hours getting back to the hostel around 4 am. Thank God! Because I only had to sleep in the grime for 2 hours.

It was a ridiculously fun night and the beginning of a friendship that has lasted to this day – though time and distance makes our connecting much less common.

"It's like golf with a 'D'," he said. And I never forgot it.

II

Kate and the Horses

It was a beautiful Sunday afternoon. I sat inside Hackett's Bar with my friend Kenny Dread, the doors wide open to let the sunshine and warmth in.

It was my first gig in Ireland and Kenny and I had prepared a jazz set to filter into the afternoon. Songs like "My Funny Valentine", "I Thought About You" and "It Don't Mean a Thing".

I was fresh from Seattle and had spent years in the jazz scene there working up the courage to sing at jams and eventually gig. Now here I was, in a remote village in Ireland, ready to become part of the gorgeous music scene that was, and still is, alive and well in West Cork.

Months later I'd discover that texts were being sent out during our sets, about this amazing new singer, and you should come down and hear her kind of thing. When I think back, I realise how special that was. And to me, that's how music goes in Ireland. It's a community thing. Something that connects, shares, and expands.

As I sat in a multicoloured hoodie, my mezzo-soprano voice floating out into the air, Kenny sat beside me drinking rosé. He was always drinking rosé. And I couldn't help but notice that my friend Jean was missing from the crowd! She knew about the gig and said she'd come, but I couldn't see her small bird body anywhere.

Meanwhile, in Kealties, Jean was entertaining her new couch surfer, Kate. Kate was from Colorado and had travelled to Ireland on her first Celtic pilgrimage. She'd felt the call to come and like most spiritual seekers took that call to heart.

They were sitting drinking tea in Jean's kitchen, chatting about life when Jean looked up at her clock and thought, blimey! "Blimey" was a totally Jean thing to say. She told Kate she'd forgotten about a very important event and that they should leave right then and there. And so they did. Jean left a hilarious voicemail on my phone letting me know they were on the way to hear me sing on that sunniest of Sundays.

But by the time they arrived, the gig was over. And what a gig it had been!

We all walked down the street to a fish and chips shop that I'm pretty sure isn't there anymore to have a celebration meal, and that's where I met Kate. Kate, the dark-haired lassie from my own country. She was hilarious. We clicked instantly.

When she mentioned that she was planning on hitchhiking to Dzogchen Beara the next day, I offered her a lift. Dzogchen Beara is a Buddhist retreat centre on the Beara Peninsula, not far outside of Castletownbere. It sits on a cliff looking out over the Atlantic, with views of the ends of the Sheep's Head and Mizen Peninsulas on a clear day. It's a truly stunning place so I was keen to see it again myself.

I picked Kate up in Bantry the next day and out we drove, along Bantry Bay, through Glengarriff and along the southern coast of the Beara Peninsula towards our destination. We couldn't stop talking. I remember feeling like I'd met a soul sister and now we were on this little adventure together in my new home. I was super happy.

As we drove the narrow streets of Castletownbere moving west towards the Buddhists, I told Kate about an all-women's BnB that I'd volunteered at years ago. We decided to pull off the road at the turning to their home and that's when we saw the entrance to Dunboy Castle. I'd heard stories about the ruins and failed mansion hotel on this property and had always been curious about what lay inside.

Kate and I checked out the beautiful, stone guardhouses on each side of the driveway, with crosses carved into the sandstone. And like the two very curious human beings that we were, decided to brave the unknown and drive down the gravel road to go exploring.

We were not disappointed.

The first thing we encountered on the long drive in were three Irish draft horses, one of which was most definitely a stallion. Kate squealed at me to stop the car. She was a horse person. She had her own horse back home and was already missing him.

She hopped out and began doing her horse whisperer thing with this gorgeous animal. She spoke to him, and his ears perked up. She stroked his black, white, and brown fur. And then the funniest thing happened. He let out the *longest* fart I have ever heard coming out of anything. It just went on and on like a traditional Irish tune. And once it completed itself, Kate and I died laughing on the side of the road. In total stitches.

We continued along, the narrow road lined with fields, and soon came upon a giant, grey Victorian Gothic mansion with fencing all around it. Originally built as a home for John Puxley and his family after the success of his business venture, the Allihies Mining Company, his son Henry added the audacity of the Victorians to it in the late 1800s. It is said the renovation of this building cost €36,872.

In 1872 Henry's wife died in childbirth and the story goes that, after the funeral, he left Ireland, never to return. The house fell into disrepair.

In 1921 the IRA burnt out the building after a rumour that English troops were meant to be housed there. 5 years later Henry Puxley sold the land to a local family and this former home lay burnt and broken until 1999 when it was sold to a consortium of hotel groups.

In 2004, with some heavy-hitting investors on board, the Puxley Mansion was slated for a restoration project worth €50 million and was set to become Ireland's only 6-star hotel.

Then they hit a surprising snag.

An endangered species of bat was discovered in the ruins, the Lesser Horseshoe Bat. The project was put on hold until a special kind of bat house was constructed nearby, built to the tune of €150,000. And, according to environmental law, the bats were not allowed to be hand moved, so the project waited again until these bats decided to make their new home in the house so lovingly built for them.

A bat the size of a plum put this massive project on hold for a month.

Finally, with the mansion restored and 72 new suites built near the back of the castle, a soft opening of the hotel was held around Christmas time in 2007. Only to have bad luck strike again!

In 2008 Ireland went into a massive financial downturn and the main financiers of the Puxley Mansion project filed for bankruptcy. The doors of this place closed once again.

So, Kate and I found the house just as it had been left in 2008. Rooms almost complete. Bathrooms full of marble tiles. And a glass walkway connecting parts of the castle. It was eerie. And beautiful. And so curious. But we knew nothing of this place's history then.

We wandered down to the sea along the entrance to the quay of Berehaven to discover another set of ruins, this time properly old. Built by the last great O'Sullivan Beare clan leader in the 1500s, it fell into ruin in 1602 after a great battle between the English and the Irish. Now it was just peace – grass and gorse flowers and the wind rippling the plant life as we wandered and explored.

As the sun began to sink lower in the sky, I drove Kate up the mountain road to Dzogchen Beara and dropped her off at the stunning views surrounding that place just in time for sunset. We had coffee and pastries at their little café and were only mildly spoken down to by the hipster Buddhists running the cash register. For some reason, there were often holier-than-thou Buddhists in there!

And then I got in my green Ford Focus from the year 2000 and drove the manual gear shift back home to the Sheep's Head.

And the Puxley Mansion? It's slated for another multi-million-euro renovation with the intention of becoming a luxury hotel. Just like in 2004. Here's hoping!

12

No Phone Joe

When I first moved to Ireland, I decided that I was going to do one handstand per day.

I was working on being able to go upside down without a wall or other vertical surface to hold me and knew the power of a simple, daily practice that I could commit to without too much effort. A little bit, every day, made for progress!

Plus, it was a spark of creativity in my day. I'd look for a beautiful, interesting, or inspiring location and sometimes ask the help of strangers to take my photo. I'd collected a cool set of stories about these encounters so far. And that's how I met Joe.

He was sitting in his small, blue van in a parking area near Glengarriff Woods. The ground around him was littered with bright red and yellow leaves from the oak and beech trees of the forest. A perfect spot for my handstand!

I didn't want to ask him to help me at first. He looked a little creepy sitting there and man, I'd already encountered some kooky people in West Cork. You just never knew what you were gonna get when you started a conversation with someone.

I'm glad I asked him though.

Joe lived up the way towards Barley Lake. He didn't own a telephone. Of any kind. And his sister, up in Tralee I think it was, had to write him letters to get in contact.

I laughed as he spoke. And there was something I noticed about him almost immediately.

He had an attention span.

This man really listened when I started sharing with him. His focus did not waiver. And when he began telling me about a recent trip to India that he took, I was taken by his slow approach to the story. How the sounds and colours and sights of India blew his mind and how the food did not – he was a meat and potatoes kind of guy it turned out. He set the scene for his nephew's wedding to an Indian woman, the weekend of events full of marigolds and excitement. He drew me in. It was such a lovely feeling.

This man was a natural storyteller.

I've noticed, especially nowadays, people are harder to talk to than they used to be. They're often busy, looking at their phone, or shifting their attention to something or someone else. It's rare to find a human who truly connects with you and takes in what you're saying. Joe did all those things.

But Joe was nervous to take my photo. He wasn't good with cameras, he said. I showed him how it worked and what I needed and wanted, and that man took a great photo of me, in the dirt parking lot, surrounded by brightly fallen leaves, holding a handstand for less than a second.

13

Howard and the Motorcycle

There were some days in Ireland that stretched me to remember why I moved there.

Like any place, when you start the real experience of living and working, difficult emotions sometimes rise up to notice and feel. And then, a moment like the one I'm about to share with you happens. Two men and a motorcycle. Suddenly it became easy to remember why I loved living there.

It was a sunny Saturday, warm by all accounts. I decided to head over to one of my favourite places near the sea to relax and play guitar. I tucked myself down off the road amongst the rocks near the pine tree and began strumming some chords, singing to myself – the pier and trees my audience. I wasn't long there when a man on a motorcycle pulled off the road and stopped. He took his helmet off and said, "Hey, will you give us a song? "

He was so cheerful, I laughed! Two minutes later his friend and riding partner showed up and they both made their way down onto the rocks around me for a private concert in the West Cork sunshine. I played two songs for them, and they smiled and clapped and encouraged me the entire time, an appreciative audience. In fact, the one on the left told me I made his day!

After a good chat, all about music and life and bikes, I finally asked what had been rising up as a desire in my heart – I asked for a ride on one of their motorcycles. I can't remember if I used the word ride or the word lift; I hope lift! In Ireland, a ride means something else entirely.

The man on the right gave me his helmet and gloves and protected my guitar, while the man on the left took me for a spin. Now it had been years, I'd say 21 of them, since I'd been on the back of a motorbike. It's such a cool feeling, all exposed and exciting, but easy and calm at the same time. We tore down the road towards Glengarriff, the heat of the bike rising off it, the heat of the man rising up into my hands. Giddy, I got off at the end, still feeling the vibrations from the engine running through my legs!

For a couple of hours, two lifelong friends (the guys had known each other since they were little) and a woman from America met on the shores of the Wild Atlantic Way and shared a set of moments that weave into all of our memories.

To me, this is beauty. This is spontaneity. And it is something that happens with ease in Ireland – a natural unfolding of life that can sometimes be perceived as lackadaisical. And maybe it is. But I'd say there's a lot of magic in that lack and something our modern world desperately needs – real connection that unfolds with ease. Surprises that we are open to. And meeting strangers with a little less fear and a little more openness.

So, thank you, Howard and Jason. It was a pleasure meeting you. Truly.

Months later Howard sent me a thank you note on Facebook. We've stayed in touch to this day. He has always encouraged me to pursue music, even when I'm off doing other things. Anyway, here's what he wrote:

"What's good! I went on my first date in 28 years, and it was great.

In short, life (or rather wife (x-wife as of last April)) has been a little cruel for about 8 years!!

And I feel a corner has just been turned. The sun is indeed brighter, and hope is restored. Karma has begun to pay out again.

Meeting you that day was one of the few wonderful moments that kept me going, and not losing faith in people altogether.

I instinctively knew you were a great person and stole a few moments with you for memories as a reminder to have faith.

Thanks, you are one of those that helped me make it through.

A song and a smile from a lovely lady lifts the heart like nothing else.

Keep singing Kat.

PS Stay away from motorbike men, they are dangerous! Thanks for the photo, send more!!"

So let this be a reminder to everyone reading now – you never know how a smile or a wave or a magic little encounter like this will impact someone. Apparently, what we do matters. Apparently, what we do can really make a difference. Stay kind. Stay open. And take care.

14

Liz and the Garda Station

I walked into the Garda Station in Bantry with trepidation.

It was time to check in with my immigration officer about renewing my visa and this appointment always made me nervous, no matter how many times I did it. I wanted to stay in the country for a longer period of time, but whether my visa would be renewed was a mystery of the universe at this moment.

The revolving doors spun me into a concrete chamber with high ceilings. Across from the door was a window with a bell next to it. With a small lump in my throat, I pressed the button letting the guards know there was a person at their counter. Can I call it a counter?

I barely noticed a woman with long black hair and a tiny baby in a car seat carrier sitting, waiting on the concrete bench. What is up with concrete in police stations? I thought to myself.

I joined them and sat down, butterflies and all, to wait and see.

The woman sitting next to me was called Liz. The moment I heard her speak I knew she was American. I'd been in Ireland long enough to get excited about hearing the voice of a person from my home country. I felt my heart beat a little faster. When she told me she was from Cape Cod outside of Boston I got even more stoked. Boston accents are the best.

As this woman and I began to open up to one another I knew instinctively that I liked her. She herself was open, honest, frank, funny, and straight up – unlike the people of my new country who had a totally different social system than I was used to. But here was a girl after my own heart!

I'll always remember that conversation because Liz helped me make a decision I'd been struggling with for some time. I wanted to stay in Ireland for sure, but I also wanted to go back to the US for a few months to see family and work as a waitress so I could supplement my income as a virtual assistant and make extra cash to pay off my debt. In the US, our service industry is tip-based. In Ireland, it is not.

It went something like this...

"So, Liz, what were you doing for work in the US before you came to Ireland?" I said.

"My husband and I are in the restaurant industry! Simon is a chef and I've been doing front of house work for ages. I also *love* wine and have worked unofficially as a sommelier."

"Woah, no way! That's so cool. And so weird. I've been thinking about going back to the States for a few months to see family and make extra money as a waitress. I really want to make a dent in my debt this year."

"Oh my god, you could totally do that." Liz said. She was so encouraging. "Simon and I had a bunch of debt we wanted to pay off before we moved over here to Ireland, so we worked wicked long hours and totally made our goal. We even saved for the trip!"

You know when you've been thinking about something for a while and then you run into a person and somehow you start talking about life and suddenly you get clarity? Yup. Thank you, Liz.

I don't know how long we talked in that grey cathedral of justice; it was probably only fifteen minutes. But I enjoyed every moment. Liz and her then husband Simon (Dublin born and bred) had moved over to Ireland for a year to try it out and see if they wanted to live abroad. Then Liz got pregnant! And sitting at her feet was their 6-week-old daughter Ava - a little meatloaf of a girl with light skin and a sweet smell. You know, that baby smell.

Liz and I exchanged numbers. Then Mauraid Cronin, our mutual red-headed immigration officer came down and called Liz's name.

Liz stood up, gave me a quick hug and grabbed Ava the meatloaf. "Goodbye Kat. So good to meet you. Let's have lunch soon!"

Not long after it was my turn to climb those same steps and meet with Mauraid. The laws around visas and immigration were in total flux those years as the local and national governments figured out how they wanted to organise things, so there was a bit of run around. But my visa was extended and I was granted another year in Ireland. I left with a happy heart. Another year and a new friend. Wow.

A few weeks later Liz and I met for lunch. It was a vibe. We made plans to go hiking the week after. Slowly, but surely, we got to know each other and then eventually became neighbours! Liz and Simon decided to move to the Sheep's Head Peninsula. I'd often walk to their house for dinner. And when the psychology of the Irish people completely befuddled us, we'd make cocktails and sit by the fire while Ava slept and get all American. It made us feel better every single time.

Eventually I had the honour of being the first person outside of the family to babysit Ava so Liz and Simon could go on a date. It was such an amazing thing to be part of the growing up of a young thing. I loved it so much and it was a welcome addition to my life in West Cork.

But one of my favourite memories was the stretch of time Liz and Simon ran a series of pop-up restaurants in Ahakista out of the Heron Gallery. The first dinner was a New Orleans-themed night. Liz and Simon had also lived in N'Olens for a year and loved their experiences there. The food, the culture, the sticky, sweaty summer heat – it had its own kind of magic. So, it felt natural to begin their series of dinners this way.

Liz asked me to waitress with her and it made me laugh. I thought back to our conversation in the Gardai station – how cool that we were now working together. Simon chefed in the kitchen preparing amuse bouches and steaming bowls of gumbo and cocktails.

The weather, in her strange way, even cooperated that May night! It was quite warm for Ireland and the wind was minimal, so the midges came out in full force. We had to close ALL the windows and doors and people were sweat-ting! I saw Irish people fanning their faces with their napkins, Mardi Gras beads round their necks. It felt like we'd been transported straight to Louisiana.

Sometimes I think about all the time Liz and I have spent together, the things we've seen and done and shared – then I look back and think, wow, who would have thought? I walked into a concrete building nervous about my legal status in Ireland and walked out with a long-term friend.

15

Robin the Herbalist

After listening to the sounds of chisels on stone and watching strong men lift big rocks during West Cork's annual Stone Symposium, I headed over to Frank's shop in a remote village on the Sheep's Head Peninsula for a popsicle.

Thankfully it's an all-in-one-shop – the popsicles are kept near the post office counter.

Only Frank wasn't there! I walked outside, popsicle in hand, and found him chatting away with a short, American sounding woman. He was filling up her car with petrol and all I kept thinking was, God, I've never actually seen that fuel pump in use!

As I stood waiting to pay, I began to observe this small woman. She had lovely, flowing hair and what seemed a natural intuition. There was something in the way she spoke to Frank that made me feel this. I unwrapped my popsicle and began to lick the cold colours to soothe the heat of the day. As I licked, I wondered – where was this woman from and what she was doing down here in Kilcrohane in late March?

You just never know who you're going to meet...

Turns out this woman was Robin Rose Bennett, a well-known herbalist, and elder in the world of medicinal plants. She is a teacher, published author, and has worked for years in the Bronx giving free health consultations to local people. And she completely surprised me outside of that shop when she asked, almost out of nowhere, "Are you Rosalee's friend?" ... My popsicle almost dropped out of my hand!

You see, the summer before, my herbalist friend Rosalee de la Forêt came on my Retreat to Ireland as a guest teacher and participant. Robin found out about me from Rosalee. For three weeks before her trip she thought about getting in touch but didn't. So, when we met in the little village of Kilcrohane on this sunny Sunday we were both surprised and excited. After some talking, we decided to spend time together and explore this fortuitous meeting.

We got in the car and drove over to the nearby Beara Peninsula. Robin would shout out little hellos or thoughts or facts about the plants we encountered – how she loved using the flowers of elderberry for medicine, how hawthorn is one of her favourite trees, and how useful self-heal is as a medicinal plant.

"Hello, Gorse! Hello Meadowsweet! Hello Fuchsia!" she yelled cheerfully out the window.

We stopped at Dzogchen Beara, the Buddhist retreat centre with an incredible view, and had lunch. Chatting amongst ourselves and the plants. Then we drove further down the coast to visit the Hag of Beara, an ancient stone that represents a Goddess in her crone years who brings winter with her wherever she goes and wields the power of life and death. People stop here to leave trinkets and gifts not only out of respect, but also as a prayer offering for their lives.

Both of us took a quiet moment by the stone, quiet except for the ever-present coastal wind. I left a 1-euro piece at the Hag's stone feet, sending a wish out into the Universe for both health and happiness, a simple prayer I'd learned years ago.

We drove the *whole way* around the Beara Peninsula, and I dropped Robin back to her car near sunset. It was a full and wholly unexpected day enjoying each other's company, exploring, and soaking the warmth of the Irish sun right into our bones. Because that's what you do in Ireland, just in case the sun doesn't return!

As I walked to the Fish Kitchen afterwards to sit down for a relaxing meal I sighed. My time in Ireland was changing me. The day had started out with a desire for a popsicle and turned into a 10-hour adventure. And what really struck me was that Robin actually had my phone number yet had never used it.

She told me that she'd reached out to my friend Rosalee before her trip because she knew Rosalee had spent time in Ireland and wanted to get some suggestions. Rosalee gave her my number with a strong urge to reach out to me and connect. The mystery of the land somehow drew us together, without her ever having to pick up the phone!

16

Wild Remedies

My friend Rosalee was raking pine needles when she decided to come on my annual retreat in Ireland.

She'd been dreaming about it for years and then two things happened – in the same week, she got two very important emails from two of her favourite redheads. One was from me announcing that the summer of 2017 would be the last time I would run my Ireland retreats. And the second was from Tori Amos. Tori was putting out her newest album, Native Invader, and going on tour with a concert in Cork City – on Rosalee's birthday. And the concert and Rosalee's birthday perfectly lined up with my retreat. She made her decision then and there.

As we passed emails back and forth that spring after the pine needle incident, a plan began to form, like honey dripping down a jar and pooling on the table. We decided she would attend as a guest instructor and partial participant. She would also leave a day early to go up to Cork because, well, Tori.

Over the course of my knowing Ireland, I ran six retreats. Six week-long adventures filled with yoga, nature, and culture in West Cork. And my all-time favourite retreat was the one I ran with Rosalee. Thank you, Tori Amos!

Rosalee is an herbalist, a published author, and an all around badass when it comes to making her living online, following her passion. She is smart and makes beautiful educational courses teaching people how to use herbs in practical, nourishing, and medicinal ways. Her courses are well-researched, backed by science and a lot of personal experience. I am so proud of her!

The moment she stepped off the plane we couldn't stop talking. I'm pretty sure we spoke non-stop, minus like 8 hours of sleeping each night, for an entire three days before the participants arrived. We went skinny-dipping, out for dinner and pints and explored some of the offerings of the Ellen Hutchins Festival, a yearly event in West Cork.

Ellen Hutchins was Ireland's first notable female botanist. She'd been unwell as a child and her doctor prescribed time in nature as a health tonic. That's how she got into botany. She discovered many new species and was the first botanist to document that some seaweeds do create their own fruit!

The festival honours her memory and celebrates botany, botanical art, and the ever-shifting beauty of the ocean in Bantry Bay. It has a wide range of events designed to encourage people of all ages to explore the natural and cultural heritage of the area. Rosalee was particularly touched by our experiences there.

This trip is also the first time I realised my friend was a bit of a rock star in the herbal world. Most of the retreat participants were from her email list and I swear, it was like they had googly eyes for her. They couldn't get enough of her teaching and sharing knowledge. It made me laugh because I'd known her since back in the day, but it also made me another level of proud that she'd worked so hard and created a following of people who respected her work.

The retreat went amazingly well, all our participants had a great time and for me, it was the first time I had an actual team assisting me. Rosalee as a guest instructor, one of my close friends at the time as a driver, and a local friend as the cook! We hiked along the Atlantic Ocean, went kayaking in bioluminescence (and made history by being the first group in *years* to have a capsize), made jewellery and even tried our hand at an old form of stone carving.

Before our participants arrived Rosalee and I decided to put together a little welcome package and made bog myrtle insect spray as one of the gifts. Bog myrtle is a beautiful aromatic shrub that grows wild in Ireland and is known for its bug-repellent properties. I'd spent a lot of time with bog myrtle in my wanderings of Ireland's wild places and it had become a favourite plant, so I was super excited by this!

We were out on the end of the Sheep's Head Peninsula when we got a chance to use our spray. Normally a windy spot, the wind died down just as we'd sat for tea and cake outside Bernie's shop after our hike. It was such a relief to have the quiet after all the howl. The respite only lasted a moment though because thousands of midges filled the air moments later and began feeding. On us.

Everyone started scrambling it was that bad, gathering layers and socks and sipping one last drink of tea. Rosalee and I looked at each other, opened up our packs as we moved towards the car, and pulled out our bog myrtle bug spray – a real moment of need. I watched as she sprayed her arm, dotted with midges. Nothing happened! The midges kept crawling around like they had been sprayed with water. I'm pretty sure our laughter rang many miles out to sea before the safety of the car doors enclosed us.

All too soon it was time for Rosalee to leave us and head up to the big city to see Tori Amos play. One of the cool things I've learned about Tori is that she spends a good portion of time meeting with her fans prior to the concert. Rosalee got in line so she could have a chance to meet her and give her a signed copy of her first published book, Alchemy of Herbs (Hay House) which had come out about a year and a half before this moment. She was number 22 in line.

One of the things that Rosalee emphasised in all our chats both pre and in Ireland was that she was NOT going to write another book, it had just been too much work. She wanted to focus her energy on creating and maintaining online courses. She was super clear. But something shifted when she met Tori.

They were together for all of five minutes. But Rosalee told me those five minutes stayed with her for days afterward – how present Tori had been, how gracious and how quick she was to turn the conversation towards Rosalee. She ended up asking a question that really stuck with my friend. She asked her, what is the best way to take herbal medicines?

In retrospect, she realised Tori was probably asking that question literally, like should a plant be eaten fresh? Taken as capsules? Powder? But Rosalee's mind expanded, and she told Tori that *the best* way was to infuse medicinal plants into aspects of your everyday life. Cook with them. Go hang out with them in your garden or in the wild. And connect with nature on a daily basis!

The next day Rosalee flew home, back to the Methow Valley in Eastern Washington.

A few days later she was standing in her kitchen, thinking obsessively about her conversation with Tori Amos (because that's what you do with your idols), when it hit her. She 100% had to write a book about bringing wild plants into your life every single day, one that highlighted how important nature connection is in general and specifically in the world of herbalism. And so *Wild Remedies* was born.

We find inspiration in the most interesting places, don't we? Rosalee had set her mind against ever writing a book again. But a trip to Ireland, learning about Ellen Hutchins and her 5 minutes with Tori Amos changed her. And that makes me so happy because I was a part of the magic and inspiration and all I'd been doing was following my intuition, drawing closer to what felt right and real and above all, fun.

Unfortunately, Ellen Hutchins was not a redhead, but Rosalee was so touched by her story she included her in the introduction to her book. Tori and I made the Acknowledgements section.

When Rosalee's book came out, she sent me a signed copy with a little note inside:

Dear Kat, In many ways you were responsible for inspiring this book! I'm looking forward to the next time we can get together and make magic. xox Rosalee

17

I See you Got the Irish in You!

Her name was Bridget. A beautiful little black woman working behind the desk at the Atlanta Hartsfield airport's Delta SkyMiles Club.

I'd walked in completely travel weary to enquire how much the cost of entering would be. I was travelling from Ireland to the US to visit family and was full of the difficulty I was having living and adjusting abroad. And I think this woman saw it.

"Hello, how much is it for a day pass?" I said.

She smiled.

"Honey, are you a Platinum or Premium Delta SkyMiles member?" she asked.

"No, no, unfortunately not," I replied.

She paused. I could tell she was thinking.

"Well, are you a Gold or Silver member then?"

"No. I'm nothing as special as that." I said, almost dejectedly.

But you could tell, this woman was an angel. And she wasn't going to let me speak to myself that way.

"Honey. You are special!" she said in her lovely southern drawl. "You are special. You know why? Because God made you special! God doesn't make anything by mistake."

I could feel a smile starting to creep over my face, pulling me out of my depths and into the present moment.

Then she looked at me square and said:

"Hmmm! Girl. I see you got the Irish in you! You know what I'm gonna do? You know what? I'm gonna make you my guest for the day. Free of charge. You just come on in, on me."

I nearly wept and laughed at the same time as she spoke. Rainbow weather in Atlanta!

And so, Bridget the travel agent shooed me on into the lounge where I sat in big comfy chairs and ate weird, but strangely good airport buffet food. I felt the weariness in my soul draw out to only weariness in my bones. The hours ticked by, and I made myself at home in Bridget's guest house.

Bridget is a very Irish name. I often wonder where her name came from. And if she too had Irish connections. I never mentioned where I was travelling from or to. *She just saw me.*

Bridget, I'm hoping that, with a little of that luck of the Irish, this book somehow finds itself in your hands. I want to thank you. I have never forgotten your kindness. You changed the course of my day. That's why you get your own little story in this story of mine.

18

Oh, Johnny, Oh!

I folded my arms across my chest and hugged them in close to help prevent an exasperated sigh from passing my lips as I waited in line.

What was taking this guy so long? I was standing, waiting to buy my bus ticket to Cork City outside Dublin Airport and the man in front of me was taking forever. I'd just returned from about 6 weeks in the States, my current irritation an indicator that I was back in a country that valued people over efficiency.

The moment I realised this I took a deep breath, relaxed, and started listening to the conversation. When I heard the man in front of me mention Bantry, I paused. That's where I was heading!

So, I did what any Sagittarius rising person with Irish ancestry and a love for people would do and struck up a conversation with this man. His name was Johnny O'Sullivan. Born and raised in the Mealagh Valley outside Bantry he now lived in Atlanta full-time as a teacher and was returning home to visit his family.

We stood and waited together after I bought my ticket and talked until the bus came. It pulled up with its classic red Irish setter logo and I heard the recorded voice of an Irishman say, "Steer clear. Luggage door is operating." Ah yes, I was truly back in Ireland!

And that could have been it between me and Johnny O. Except it wasn't.

Three and a half hours later we pulled into the Bus Eireann station at Parnell Place and disembarked, my eyes crusted with sleep. It was a cool and sunny day in the city, and I was waiting for my friend Ger to come down and collect me. I'd parked my car at his place and still had a two-hour drive to get myself home.

When I saw Johnny on the pavement the words flew out of my mouth before I had a chance to think:

"Hey, I'm headed down towards Bantry today and have my car up here in Cork. Do you want a lift down with me?"

Of course he did. No one *wants* to ride the bus in Ireland.

Then, the funniest little set of events started happening. My friend Ger arrived. Ger met Johnny, heard the new plan, and suddenly we were all going to get coffee together. Johnny had to go meet his sister for a moment (she worked at a clothing shop in the city) and said he would meet us for coffee after. Ger and I walked down the cobblestone streets towards Starbucks, just around the corner from H&M. I peered into the windows, curious at what kinds of clothes were found in an *Irish* H&M.

And then we were all in Starbucks! Drinking flat whites and laughing like we'd known each other for ages. Johnny wore a green sweater, his eyes flashing with mischief as so many Irish eyes tend to do. And I thought, what would have happened if I hadn't taken a deep breath at the bus station? Or just let those words escape my mouth. This moment would never have happened!

This is Ireland my friends. Strangers become friends at the drop of a hat.

I drove Johnny home that day. His family invited me in for dinner and I joined them for a Sunday roast. The table was full of food and people, so many siblings! They are a boisterous family which was a new experience for me in Ireland and one that I loved.

Johnny and I have been in touch ever since.

19

Susan the Fiddler

It was a chilly autumn night and I was in the town of Doolin in County Clare – known for its live music and close proximity to the Cliffs of Moher.

The Cliffs are a UNESCO Global Geopark and a huge tourist attraction. Standing at about 700 feet high, they are made from sandstone and shale, creating homes for a plethora of sea birds.

I'd just finished helping an American ethnobotanist run a 2-week retreat in Ireland and decided to spend a couple of extra days up the country in this special place, relaxing. In a glamping yurt!

I was debating about skipping dinner and just staying cosy in bed, but I decided to brave the chill and head out. I drove Doolin's two main streets, looking for inspiration, and finally settled on Fitzpatrick's.

This place has a fine dining restaurant and pub with a hotel attached to it. The tables were set with lovely candles and the atmosphere was quiet, just what I'd been wanting! Unfortunately, the wait time was over an hour, so I decided to head into the pub, sit at the bar and eventually order.

It's funny. There are all these little moments in life when we make decisions. Even micro decisions. And we don't always realise how, should we have chosen anything else, our night would have turned out completely differently. Well, tonight was one of those nights where I remembered this truth.

My food came and I began to dig in, the sounds of Ireland all around me in the form of laughter, the chat, and the music floating from the band out in front of me. As a traveller, it's one of those series of moments that really stick out – where you're fully immersed in a culture, eating their food, listening to their music, and drinking their beer.

My plate empty, I began to focus on the music and turned my barstool towards the players. They were a trio comprised of guitar, fiddle, and banjo, a very rare combination in my experience of Ireland. A few minutes later the front door of the pub opened and a woman with glasses came in. She registered in my mind enough to really have a look.

Here's what it sounded like in my head:

"God, she looks familiar! Wait, do I know her? Wait ... what? Oh my god!"

"*Susan?*" I said out loud, aiming my voice in her direction.

And wouldn't you know it, but there stood Susan Burke.

I met Susan when I lived out in the Pacific NW in Washington state and was a student and later an employee of Wilderness Awareness School. She had a beautiful home just down the road from some land the school owned. Eventually, I started doing odd jobs for her, like house cleaning or weeding. She was a red-headed fiddle player who specialised in playing Irish music! And now here she was, on vacation in Doolin, the Irish music capital. Of course she was here!

Susan and I hadn't seen each other in years except occasionally on social media. So the look of surprise and then delight on her face was palpable. We wrapped each other in a warm hug and spent the rest of the night going from pub to pub, listening to Irish music.

It felt like kismet.

Did you know that the word kismet has roots in both the Arabic and Turkish languages? It also has ties to Islam and means the pre-divined fate of Allah. It arrived into the English language in the late 1800s and began to take on the meaning of fate or destiny, untied from any particular God. This experience felt so much like that!

A couple years after this meeting Susan and I exchanged the following messages:

Me: Happy Birthday Susan

Still amazes me that we ran into each other in Doolin!

Susan: LOL

It was miraculous!!!

20

So Much Time, So Little to Do

I picked up a small piece of white chalk and began writing on her mini chalkboard in the kitchen, right under the yellow printed words Shopping List: *So much time, so little to do... 087-755-6732*

It must have been 2015 when I wrote those words along with my phone number. And the chalkboard stayed that way until the day she died in November 2021.

How do I begin to tell you about Jean? It's hard to know where to start with a friendship that spanned 12 years and an age gap of forty. So I guess I'll start at the very beginning.

I met Jean on accident. I was travelling in Ireland for the first time and found myself volunteering at a place that did not live up to its online appearance. A week in I began researching other options and settled on attending a Jazz Festival (whose existence completely surprised me) in the small village of Ballydehob. My next step was to find a place to stay.

A friend of mine told me about a website called couchsurfing.org – a free connecting service that puts travellers in touch with locals as a form of hospitality and cultural exchange. Most people on the site offered actual beds to sleep in, so surfing the couches wasn't even always an option! And that's where I met Jean.

"My name is Jean, so when you write to me, please include my name. Although I am slightly older than most Couch Surfers, I am very young at heart and young in spirit. I get on well with and am able to liaise with people of all ages.

When I was 19/20, I hitch-hiked around almost all countries (then) of central Europe. I met the guy I was to later marry on a pedestrian bridge crossing the River Rhine in Germany. He was serving with the British Forces Overseas.

More recently, before coming to live in Ireland, I circumnavigated the island of Ireland by motorbike.

I am widowed for the last eight years but have now got the travelling bug back again!"

Her profile said she was 60 years old. Wow.

I messaged Jean and she came back to me straight away. While practically speaking, staying with her to attend the festival would be tricky, we did agree to meet at a car boot sale during the festival (Jean *loved* car boot sales). And that's how we became friends.

Over the years I visited her many times, as both a couch surfer, WOOFER (World Wide Opportunities on Organic Farms), and later just because. Just because we liked each other's company.

One of our rituals became the annual cutting of the hedges surrounding her green cottage. She would get out her electric cutter and I would woman the wheelbarrow, taking all the bits and pieces of rose and butterfly bush, fuchsia, and unnamed greenery to the 'municipal dump' – a spot about 40 metres down the road, carved into the grasses by all the workers before me, right down onto the beginning of the bog. I must have walked that trail hundreds of times over the years.

But the very first time we cut Jean's hedges was the most memorable.

It was a warm day for Ireland. The sun was shining brightly, illuminating the patchworked green fields, Dunmanus Bay sparkling in the distance. I'd just returned from the dump when all of a sudden, I saw Jean. And then I didn't. She disappeared. All 5 foot 4 of her.

The details are a bit fuzzy on what happened next. But not long after her disappearance I grabbed my camera and began filming.

You see, Jean had fallen into a hole in the hedge. The electric trimmer went in with her too. She was unharmed. On a slope. And took ages to right herself. I threw her a pair of gardening gloves to ease the poking, while Anke, another guest at Jean's, joked about us heading down to the pub and we'd see her later.

Jean, however, was unphased. Her distinct English accent rose up out of the hawthorn and bright pink, fuchsia flower hole, "While I'm here I'm going to jolly well cut those bits down!"

And when she stood, she did. That was Jean.

Saturdays were her weekly crossword puzzle parties with a couple of the other local ladies on the Sheep's Head. They'd gather in the afternoon, often in Jean's conservatory, with books and encyclopaedias, shunning technology in favour of inner knowledge and bound paper. Jean would put the kettle on and soon the women would be talking and figuring, gossiping, and laughing. And boy was their gossip stiff. I can still remember, to this day, being both intrigued and astonished at the knowledge they all possessed. I'd come to find out this was indicative of most small towns the world over. But I guess the Irish ones had a special smallness to them. Being an island that time often forgot.

Not only was Jean a crossword lover, but she was also a heart-breaker and had ignored the likes of Colin Farrell's attention!

But one of my most favourite things about Jean was how we could sit together. Reading. Or basking in the sun. Sipping on tea. And say absolutely nothing, yet still feel so connected and relaxed. I can remember baking in the sun in her conservatory, sitting in her big round chair while she sat on the couch, her black lab William at her feet. The air would get that deep quiet feeling, the kind that wraps around you and relaxes you down to your very core. It would be so quiet you could hear the bees making their rounds among the roses, or the wind moving through the willows near the stream. We'd say nothing. And I loved every moment of it.

But when Jean and I did talk? We spoke about everything. And I mean everything. You might wonder what we would have in common, two women with 40 years between them? She would tell stories about her travels and encounters with people from all over the world. Or how she fixed her front door or was planning on buying a camper van. She had a knack for discovering the highest quality charity shop finds and she never hesitated to help an animal in need. And me? I shared my adventures in dating with her. My own travel and people stories. And we constantly found new places to go and explore together.

We road-tripped to the Burren, camped at a hostel by a stream, sleeping in a very old army style tent and walked along the Cliffs of Moher to the visitor's center from a village nearby. We hitchhiked together. We explored places like the Caha Pass, Tomie's Woods (and the crazy Irish farmer guardian that came with it), the winding roads leading to Gleninchaquin, and the fields and wild lands surrounding her home. We used to use her multi-purple coloured coat to cross barbed wire fences and had a way of finding our path forward together, even when we got lost.

In November of 2021, I was living in Cape Town, South Africa, and had a trip back to Ireland planned for March 2022, with some time set aside to see Jean. I was so excited.

One night I fell asleep on the brown leather couch in my apartment and around midnight the kitchen window that faces Table Mountain flew open and woke me straight from the depths of sleep.

The wind was rushing in as I walked over, still half asleep, and managed to close it and return to the quiet of the room. That's when I looked at my phone.

A message from a mutual friend of Jean's had come through asking if I knew where she was. Apparently, she was missing.

I spent the next 24 hours making phone calls and putting up social media posts. The Facebook post I put out was shared 480 times – for all my varying opinions about social media, this reminded me of the power of it and I was super grateful to everyone who was looking out for her in West Cork.

The next morning, I woke up to a strange half-awake, half-asleep dream. I saw waves lapping. And kelp. And I had this sinking feeling that Jean was dead.

I still hadn't heard any news from Ireland, so I pulled myself together and went surfing. I had fallen in love with the sport and spent many weekends in the ocean on a longboard, learning to ride. I knew Jean would have wanted it that way. For me to be *living*. And I decided to take a surf in her honour.

While I was out in the cool waters of Muizenberg and False Bay I had another little vision. I saw Jean, smiling so big, with people all around her, like the people who had been searching for her, and for a moment I felt this surge of energy – she's alive!

But a couple hours later I found that was not the case. Jean's body was found at the base of an incredibly high cliff towards the end of the Sheep's Head Peninsula that morning. A friend of mine was actually on the rescue crew which brought me a level of comfort and gratitude. And I had this feeling that the vision I'd received of her smiling was a message from her spirit, finally free, and happy beyond measure.

I'd come to find out that Jean committed suicide. I'd never had anyone in my life commit suicide before and while I wondered if I could have done anything to help create a different outcome, I did feel a deep level of respect for Jean's choice. She was almost 81 years old when she passed away and, in my opinion, anyone that has lived that long has a right to choose how they pass.

I loved her so very much. And in the aftermath of her passing, I was told, by multiple people, that she loved me too. Each time I remember her I'm transported back to Ireland. To her green cottage. To the polytunnel her WOOFERs helped her build that filled with grapes every summer. To the spot by the sea that she loved to walk beside and the fields above her home that we wandered together.

I miss you, Jean.

21

Borlin Valley Hares

H e climbed down out of the Western Red Cedar tree and walked towards me.

I found myself holding my breath. He was so handsome. Tall and tan. Smelling of cedar fronds, wood chips and diesel. My whole body started to soften and turn light, like giggling, like floating, like a flush.

He asked me out to dinner. And at my prompting wrote his phone number on my hand:

CIAN 085-7**-6***.

I went weak.

Western Red Cedar trees are known as the Tree of Life in the Pacific Northwest. The bark is a similar colour to my own hair, fronds fragrant with a scent that hits you right in the heart and makes you take a deep breath. It's used by the Native American peoples of Washington, Oregon and British Columbia to make canoes, baskets, clothing, fishing nets, medicine and so much more. Cedar is also used as a cleansing smoke in ceremonies. The sweetness of its scent is said to purify the air, drawing in positive energy and helping people become more resilient in the face of their challenges. So imagine my surprise when I found this very tree in Ireland and this man in its highest branches.

With a Cian tattoo, I got in the car and drove straight to the Borlin Valley. Back then I was just beginning to learn how to follow my intuition. And my intuition said, go that way.

This valley is a special valley. An alternative route to Kenmare from Bantry, the roads are tiny and very steep in places. And the scenery? Peaceful. Wild. Almost otherworldly. From the moment I discovered this place I was intrigued and spent lots of hours exploring her hillsides, lakes and side roads. Hiking, driving and sitting on hilltops, singing to the wind.

I guess Cian intrigued me too. Maybe that's why I was pulled out Borlin Way?

I drove up the mountain right to the top where the counties of Cork and Kerry meet and decided to pull off the road, climb a style over the fence and walk along a path I could see on the other side. I'd always wondered about this spot but had never taken the time to stop.

It was windy, the clouds coming and going across the sun. They created cloud shadows on the earth followed by moments of big brightness only to return to darkness once again. A curious day.

As I walked along the soggy ground, I thought back to Cian. He'd smelled like diesel and woodchips. He'd written his number on my hand with a pen I gave him. I'd felt like an absolute schoolgirl in his presence, but in a way that felt good. I felt alive.

He was a mystery to me.

I made my way around the hillside and stopped, awestruck. There, to my surprise, tucked down in the valley, was a lake. Water came trickling down the cliff rocks from 100 feet above, making a seasonal waterfall.

This was Lough Nambrackderg or Lake of the Red Trout.

The lake was formed during the last ice age as glaciers moved downhill, slipping and rotating, grinding the earth away. Once the glaciers melted, these hollows filled, and Lough Nambrackderg was born. Set in the Shehy Mountains or Cnoic na Seithe in Irish, meaning Hills of the Animal Hides, it felt like being transported back in time. Like Claire in Outlander, touching a big standing stone and suddenly returning to the 1700s in Scotland. Only I just rounded a bend.

My shoes sank into the soaked earth as I walked down towards the lake. Then something caught my eye.

A murder scene.

There, strewn across the ground, were the many parts of an Irish Hare.

The Irish Hare is an ancient creature, carbon-dated fossils showing they were present in Ireland as far back as 28,000 BC. Born fully furred with their eyes open, Hares are fast, long-distance runners and live in open-ground nests or forms, not underground like other members of their scientific family. During the mating season, females will fight or box unwanted attempts from males they just aren't that into. They are fascinating creatures. And I've been surprised by them and their large bodies rounding a bend or two while living in Ireland.

In folkloric memory, shapeshifters were often said to take the form of the hare. There's a legend about Oisin, the Celtic warrior. He hunted a hare, wounding it in the leg. Oisin followed it into a thicket where he found a door leading down into the ground. He entered the burrow and came to a large hall where a beautiful young woman sat on a throne, bleeding from a leg wound.

The first thing I noticed about this hare? Its body was crumpled in a heap. I saw grey and white fur, pink and red muscle and lots of bone. Its head was still intact, eyes staring lifelessly.

Then there were the guts.

A pile of organs some distance away from the body, with the intestines strung out from the pile in a strangely neat line and then a heap.

It's hard to explain what happened next.

I had this knowing. It was about Cian. That should I proceed with this connection I was going to learn about myself from the inside out. Nothing was going to be left behind. Everything was going to be revealed. And it was going to take guts.

I wandered away from the hare and sat down on a little tuft of earth, still above the Lake of the Red Trout. I watched as the clouds covered the sun, the wind blowing hard and creating these jets of black ink across the water's surface. Then the clouds would pass and the sun would shine brightly, the blowing wind now turning those dark black jets into luminous sparkling ones. A dance of dark and light, back and forth, as the weather system moved through the Borlin Valley. It was magnificent.

I've got a question for you, my reader. Who the fuck sees all of these things, a dead hare, the wildness of the dark and light and thinks, hmmmm, yeah, maybe I should call this man?

Well, I did. And upon reflection, there is one main reason why.

4 years before this event in the Borlin, I'd had an accidental Kundalini awakening. I was sitting on my couch, working on my computer, staring out at the Snoqualmie Valley, when all of a sudden, I felt something. It was like pure pleasure. The energy started in my pelvis and as it grew it moved up the length of my spine and out of the top of my head. It felt orgasmic and it was the first time in my life I'd felt any sensations like this outside of sex.

It also wreaked havoc and was the instigator of beautiful magic in my life. A true, mixed blessing for me.

After it happened, I began to research more about how these awakenings occur. And what I found scared me. There were a lot of weird people with crazy ideas about this whole experience and I just wasn't into it. Nothing felt right. And then I found a very comforting man online. He looked like he grew up playing (and still might) Dungeons and Dragons. His voice was calm and clear and he suddenly made the whole experience feel, well, normal.

He said there were four things you needed to have a Kundalini awakening:

1. Increased vital energy in the lower abdomen and pelvis or in the entire body including the pelvis, often from long deep breathing.

2. Amplified emotions like devotion, love, release, fear or anger. Any profound opening of emotion could cause it.

3. Something must draw this energy into the central column or channel of the body. Focus is the tool. Like focusing on the sensations as they build.

4. The energy has to be circulated, things have to open up, and tensions and congestions need to be alleviated. (Tao Semko)

Relief! Suddenly this profound and mysterious experience made sense to me. I was practising and teaching lots of yoga at the time. I was also doing acupuncture and network chiropractics, both forms of healing work that had me connected to, experiencing, witnessing and cultivating energy in my body. And the amplified emotion? It was profound love. For a friend of mine.

For years after my awakening and sometimes still, to this day, it seems life conspires to teach me the lessons I most need to learn. So when I saw the light show and hare in the Borlin Valley, it seemed my spiritual path was leading me this way. Of course, I should message Cian.

At this time in my life, I was also on a quest for true love, another by-product of the Kundalini awakening. It was a question I couldn't get out of my head. What is true love? I used to ask friends, family and strangers alike this question and the answers I got were all really interesting.

But Cian's was the only one that hit my heart.

Eventually, this man and I became friends. So I asked him one night:

"C, what is true love?"

He paused for a moment as he drove, eyes fixed on the road ahead, his thin lips tightening in thought.

"True love, I think, is trust, friendship and forgiveness."

The air went still and silent as his words sunk into my being. Down into my soul.

Trust. Friendship. Forgiveness.

I sit here writing now and he is one of a handful of people that I still haven't forgiven. I've started to. The kind of forgiveness you give to the soul, not to the person. The course of our friendship was indeed mirrored at the lake in the Borlin Valley. An omen. A natural prophecy. Some Celtic magic. And I often wonder about that day. Was it a sign to move forward? A warning of what was to come? Or a simple reflection of what would most likely occur should I decide to walk that path towards him?

Now I realise I always had a choice. But back then I was so new to the spiritual path that I thought an experience like that meant 'This is for you, Kat'.

And I understand why.

Kundalini is life force. It's powerful. Electric. Primal. Strong. Intelligent.

There's a level of surrender needed to weather the storms should you not be fully prepared.

I most certainly wasn't prepared. I was simply open, curious, and a tad bit foolish. Unknowingly, I had all the ingredients necessary for its awakening.

And so, Cian, the Borlin Valley and my Kundalini Awakening are all tied together, on some level forever. Like a Celtic true love knot.

Landscapes

"And drive back home, still with nothing to say

Except that now you will uncode all landscapes

By this: things founded clean on their own shapes,

Water and ground in their extremity."

-Seamus Heaney

I fall in love with landscapes. I've come to discover this isn't normal. And do you know what? It surprises me how many people this puzzles. Because to me, befriending the natural world is one of the best decisions I've ever made in my life. Nature is honest. It's raw. And unspeakably beautiful.

As a traveller, the natural world of Ireland was my safe space and refuge for many years. And somewhere deep inside me I knew it was one of the homes of my heart.

22

Piers

One year, for my birthday, my friend Rachael gave me a pair of gloves. When I opened them, I gasped quietly. They were beautiful!

Fingerless and woven from wool somewhere between dark teal and midnight blue. Inside they were lined with fleece. They are, to this day, the best gloves I have ever owned.

When I moved to Ireland, they came with me.

One cold spring day after a hot and sweaty 6 hours working, I drove over to Snave Pier to decompress. I don't know why it became my favourite place. Maybe it was the way the landscape curved in and out there. Or the way sunrise and sunset coloured the waters all shades of purple, gold, pink, and orange. Maybe it was the lone pine tree growing on a rock island. I'm not sure. It felt a peaceful place. A place to dream and relax. And swim when the mood struck me.

But on this occasion, it did not strike. I was new to this part of the coast and nervous about getting in on my own. So I sat on the edge, letting the wind whip me, my legs dangling, releasing all the conversations, frustrations, and busyness of the day out to sea.

Back then Snave Pier wasn't very busy. Except sometimes in the summer. Nowadays they've made safety and picnicking improvements so it's harder to get a quiet moment to yourself. I was lucky back then. I liked it better back then. When there was no metal barrier between me and the edge.

I pulled my gloves off carelessly as I sat and laid them beside me. I was listening to music. Probably dreaming about some cute guy. And breathing in and out, like the motion of saltwater pushing kelp against the concrete and rock pier. Powerful. Not like a man hitting something. More fluid, like a woman giving birth.

Then the wind picked up. And I watched as one of my beautiful, dark teal gloves rolled like a tumbleweed into the dark waters. I cried out. I ran to the edge. I contemplated jumping in after it but couldn't find the nerve. And I watched as the glove floated away from me, towards the steep retaining wall, and out of rescues reach.

I flew back and grabbed my other glove. Safe! And returned to watch with disappointment the other's journey. A sacrifice to the sea.

I don't know why this story sticks out in my memory. But it's vivid. Perhaps because it was the beginning of my love affair with this place. As the years passed, I would return many times. I'd pull over to talk to family and friends from my car when the signal at home was bad. I'd keep the car running on cold days (and nights), heat blazing and jump in the sea, then run back and tuck myself inside. There were picnics and mobile hot tub days, deep conversations, and loads of jokes. And lots of watching. Watching the waves. The sun. The clouds. The weather. The movement of life. The stars in the dark of the night sky.

Sometimes after a particularly meaningful day or event, I'd go there and just sit. Breathe. And feel the magic and the mystery that is life. It's nothing like a Disney movie. It's actually really quiet. Open. Sometimes satiating. Sometimes a little wild.

It's the first place I listened to Patrick Watson's song Lighthouse. And the place that made sense of his lyrics:

Leave a light on in the wild

It's hard coming in a little blind

There's another pier I fell in love with. Farther down the N71 and out towards the Beara Peninsula. An inconspicuous white sign with black lettering that says Zetland. The road curves down in a classic Irish, one-lane style towards the sea with sweeping views of Bantry Bay and the Sheep's Head Peninsula. As you drive you pass farmyards and abandoned stone houses, the whole time going down. Then you round a blind corner and suddenly there she is.

Zetland Pier. Ooooh, the water is cold!

I first heard about this place through a neighbour of my friend Jean. She said she loved to go there and swim. There was a fine sandy beach, perfect for setting up a little camp and venturing into the ocean. I immediately knew I wanted to go there. So one day, as was her way, Jean took me. Jean Williams. She introduced me to so many things for the first time in West Cork.

There's a little gate just past the pier, down the road, rusted with age. And the path takes you to that small, white sandy beach and some large rocks, flat-topped, that are perfect for sitting. I had a fire here once, my first autumn in West Cork.

I'd set the intention to let go of some things that were weighing heavy on me, and I asked my friend Cian to come and start the fire. I can still remember when he arrived. The light was just beginning to set, and we hugged after he got out of the car. The hug was one of those timeless moments where you feel the sun, hear the birds, and feel the closeness.

And then off he went to gather sally and make a blaze.

Before he left me to my peace, I asked for a blessing. And while I can't fully remember what he said, I can remember how it made me feel with crystal clarity. As he spoke, I felt like he was speaking to me personally, but somehow the words were also simultaneously universal, like they were a message for everyone. I remember his words made me feel completely safe, protected, and loved, so much so that when he left, I wondered why I was even having a fire and what did I need to let go of again? Such is the power of love.

There is also an island off Zetland Pier, less than half a mile or about 800 metres offshore. Named Sheelane Island, it's owned by the Lovell family. Bernard Lovell was a famous British physicist and radio astronomer with family ties to Ireland. He always loved West Cork and decided to purchase the land as a vacation spot for himself and his family.

One day, I decided to swim there.

The waters at Zetland are clear. And cold. I was nervous to swim across alone, but I never noticed a strong pull in the tides there or any massive current. I really wanted the challenge.

I arrived on the island breathless. Invigorated. And full of an excitement that comes from doing something you've never done before. Something with an element of danger. And man did I need to rest!

I explored the island a tiny bit, but it being a private island and there being a boat docked around the side, I decided to stop and stay near shore, resting till I felt strong enough to swim back.

This is another place I'd come just to dream and think. I saw many things here too. Seals swimming. My friend Jean's black lab (William) begging picnickers for snacks and getting a hot dog. He gobbled that thing so fast! My retreat participants swimming and exploring the waters at low tide.

But looking back there are so many things I didn't see! For instance, the rich marine life that lives in Glengarriff Harbor and Bantry Bay. Marine invertebrates like brittle stars and feather stars. Mammals like the harbour porpoise, a year-round resident or common dolphins who move closer to shore in early summer through to September. The waters here are so full of life.

These were two of my favourite West Cork piers. I visited a few others who shall remain nameless. They are off the beaten path and should only be available to a true traveller who takes the time to speak with local people and discover local secrets. But Snave and Zetland, I'll give you these. If you ever visit West Cork, bring a picnic from Manning's Emporium or one of the local food trucks and take yourself there on a sunny afternoon. You will not regret it.

23

The Stone on the Hill

The stone sat on the hilltop like a beacon. I only happened to notice it because I turned my head to the right to feel the breeze.

It was coming off the ocean on Snave Pier, the sound of the salty waves lapping. My eyes shifted upwards and there it sat, like a beautiful surprise.

"A standing stone!", was the first thought in my head. I'd sat there so many times, how had I never noticed it before? It totally surprised and delighted me. I'd sat for many hours on this pier watching and listening, sometimes with headphones in my ears playing Coldplay and other new bands a new friend was sending me. But I'd never seen this stone.

My second thought was, "I want to find it." I promised myself that as soon as I had a stretch of time, I'd do some exploring.

Days passed. I drove to work. After work, I drove to Snave Pier to chill out. And every time I drove, I'd keep an eye out for that stone, looking for it on the horizon. I discovered there were a lot of places I could see it as I drove from Bantry to Snave, coming in and out of view along the ocean road. I started to create an investigatory map in my mind of the roads and areas that might lead to it. So I could actually touch it. And see what it saw.

Finally, my schedule opened up and the day came to find the standing stone on the hill. I was stoked. I jumped in my Ford and began driving some of the backroads from my mind map, near and right underneath the stone. There was one particular hill that looked promising. I found a road that traversed it, but it dead ended on private property. I wound my way under that stone for at least an hour. There were so many one-lane roads to check out, but still, nothing.

So I gave up.

Man, I was disappointed! I decided to drive down a road nearby and blow off some of that disappointment. As I crossed the Coomhola River and wound towards the Priest's Leap bridge I saw a sign. No, not a magic sign from the Gods, but a literal sign.

It said *Coorycommane Loop 5km.*

My mood immediately shifted! Well at least after all of this I could get a hike in.

I parked my car and began walking. The path led up a stony hill next to someone's home and continued up and up, into a planted, monocrop fir forest. When the views began to open again, a stile appeared. I climbed up and over and began ascending a boggy hill with beautiful scenery all around me.

Sweating and somewhere between lost in thought and enjoying the expansiveness I reached the crest of the hill and guess what

I found? The standing stone. Right there. On the trail. Right in front of me.

I started laughing.

It struck me that the moment I gave up my search and went with the flow I ended up finding what I was looking for.

I had been so frustrated and disappointed that to actually have found the stone was pure magic. I stood beside it and looked out at the sea, the stone a foot or two above me. My hands touched its rough, lichen-covered surface.

I could see Bantry Bay shimmering, the windy North side of the Sheep's Head Peninsula in the distance. And protected Glengarriff Bay off to the northwest where I'd sometimes go swimming with the seals. The boggy uneven ground spread out before me like a grassy blanket and the wind blew my hair every which way. Wow. What a moment.

I took pictures and messaged my magic misadventure story to a few close friends. Everyone seemed to revel in my discovery and laugh at the strange synchronicity of me and this standing stone.

I continued on, the grassy, boggy ground soggy and squishy beneath my feet from the recent rains. I crossed the hillside and climbed over another stile. Just on the other side I noticed a small plant nestled in the earth. It had sticky-looking yellow leaves. Butterwort! A carnivorous plant common in West Cork. It loves wet areas and was used long ago to help curdle milk to create a fermented drink.

The trail became rockier and eventually led to the road below and back to my starting place, passing farms, lakes, and forests along the way. I was enjoying myself immensely and truly struck by the turn of events. I sat down in my car, famished, happy, and still in awe. It felt like a beautiful life lesson to put into my library. A reminder that, sometimes, letting go gets you exactly where you want to be. Yeah, that was it. Then I started the car and drove home to get a snack.

24

Barley Lake

This isn't a story about a fantastic waterfall or water skiing with the Prince of Wales or travelling to a remote island in Tahiti to swim with sea turtles.

This is a much simpler story. It's a story that starts in County Cork near the border of County Kerry. It starts with a place called Barley Lake.

Travelling in Ireland has taught me many things and here's one that matters to this tale – small, unobtrusive signs usually lead to interesting finds. Let me say that another way – follow the little signs, they will lead you to really cool places!

That's the case with Barley Lake. Heading out of Glengarriff Village towards Kenmare you'll pass a Nature Reserve. Keep going. Not too much further along there is a brown sign with white lettering indicating a left turning for Barley Lake. Follow this winding road until you see another plain sign. And then another. The road is leading you into wilder places, so trust that another sign will appear. In this case, it will. That is not always the case in Ireland.

My relationship with this place has slowly deepened over the years. But it wasn't until I moved to Ireland in February of 2015 that it blossomed, and I began to know first-hand what a true gem this mountain lake was.

I liked to go to Barley Lake when I felt restless. When the stars were pulling at my hair again as Anais Nin said. I would park my car at the base of the last stretch of road and walk up the steep tarmac, breathing heavily as I climbed.

There were mountains all around me, almost just as many as there were sheep, staring curiously at me as they munched on green grass. It seemed there was always wind up there. And the clouds rushed over the landscape intermingling with the sun and wind, creating the most gorgeous and interesting shadows and light show.

At the crest of the hill is a small parking area and, surprise, another simple sign indicating that Barley Lake, though not yet visible, is just ahead. She sits in a large bowl amongst the mountains. Rocks and bog and grasses surround her too. There is an ancient feeling I get here, sunning on the rocks above. And a deep stillness.

Barley Lake is an ice age corrie lake, sculpted and created by the movements of glaciers. She sits 300 hundred feet above sea level, but when you're at her shores you'd never know it.

Above her shores though? You can see Glengarriff Harbor and the larger Bantry Bay, which adds to the feeling of the ancient. You are literally above the hustle and bustle of village life; and you get that big picture overview of the landscape. Easier to find wisdom, peace and calm. This place is such a gift.

The lake herself ripples in the wind, beckoning the brave to come and take a swim, though I've never been brave enough to put my feet in the tannin muck. Some people go there to fish. And others circumnavigate it, traversing the boggy, mountainous ground.

I loved this place so much that I even started writing a song about it with John Spillane. John is an iconic Irish singer-songwriter. He was an Irish language teacher for years and years, doing music as a second career. And then sometime in his forties he found commercial success and has been involved in many different kinds of musical projects. I found him inspiring and interesting, and I loved a few of his tunes. So when I found out that he was offering a songwriting workshop during Bantry's yearly Literary Festival I jumped at the opportunity to study with him. He was a great teacher and constantly reminded us that our songwriting skills would only grow and evolve with a lot of love or miracle grow as he called it.

One day we all found a quiet corner to work out some song lyrics and then bring them back to the group to perform. I didn't feel confident playing guitar and singing, so John ended up improvising with me as I sang. It was a melancholy, beautiful tune.

Here are the lyrics I wrote that day:

Come sit awhile

Above your troubles and worries

Come sit awhile

Through your troubles and cares

And we'll sit awhile, near the shores of Barley

Oh we'll sit awhile, above Bantry Bay

Barely, barley touching

Oh barely, so close to your knee

Barely, near the shores of Barley

Oh won't you come, come to me

I'm so glad I followed all those little signs and discovered this place. I fall in love with landscapes, remember? And Barley Lake was easy to love. Some people don't understand this kind of loving. How can you love land? For me it's a natural thing – the vistas, the scents of plants found there, the feel of wind, they all combine to form a connection. And the more time I spent there, the more of a relationship I formed.

Barley Lake is a home place. People have made their home in the valleys nearby. Sheep graze and wild animals nest and breed and roam there. And me? I sat. Had so many private conversations with myself. And I wandered and explored. That's where the love came from.

25

Carrauntoohil

I remember the wind. It was blowing incredibly hard, the promised clear and sunny weather making quick peeks through the cloud cover.

I remember we walked into the wind and laughed. And I remember that you were sceptical about our plans, while I felt like everything would be fine. And we decided we'd walk and see how far we could make it.

We'd gone to climb Carrauntoohil, Ireland's highest mountain. And neither of us knew what we were doing!

I'd read online about how to access the mountain. The Devil's Ladder, though ominous in name, seemed the most direct way to the top. And you were going off my word.

I remember you telling me you began to relax the moment after we met those wind-blown mountain men. They told us they'd been to the top and all had been well. I remember wind and mist sweeping through me on the saddle of the mountain as you climbed ahead of me. I remember we met a woman in her 70s, dressed all in white. She was making the climb for the first time on her own. She had a walking stick. And a lot of gumption.

Carrauntoohil rises 3,406 feet (or 1,038 metres) above Cronin's Yard, the traditional starting point for the climb. Sometime in the 1950s, a wooden cross was put on the summit of the mountain. 1976 saw it replaced with steel. And in 2014 someone cut it down as a protest against the Catholic Church.

It was very quickly replaced.

But I didn't know any of this then. I just wanted to climb the mountain with you.

I remember you were wearing your red, down coat. I remember being embarrassed about how slow I was going and then I remember thinking, fuck it. I remember sweat, and mud on my bright orange-pink shoes. I remember really enjoying being with you. And also being alone. I remember helping you carry your backpack; heavy with some ridiculously cool rock you picked up on your way down. It was so fucking heavy. And it got to the point where I just couldn't carry it anymore, even though I wanted to. I loved seeing you so free. But then again, it was your choice to bring the rock home.

When we reached the summit, you took a photo of me doing a handstand by the cross. Everyone stared, but I didn't care. I was on a mission to go upside down every day and this was a class spot to get a photo. Afterward we huddled in a 3-sided shelter, eating snacks and waiting for the clouds to clear. And they did. For a minute or two we finally got to see the other peaks and valleys of the Macgillycuddy Reeks, dotted with sheep and the long stretches of stonewalls across the landscape.

I remember it was a long way back. I remember stopping for snacks and I fell on my ass in the mud! And I remember meeting a man by the parking lot who'd bagged every peak in the area. But when I asked him if he wanted to go upside down with me, he wouldn't try it. I remember the quiet and contentment I felt as we listened to music and drove out toward Killarney for dinner.

I don't think I realised what a special place we'd just been to until the day after our trip. In the future, I'd return. Sometimes alone. Sometimes with you. There was a deep peace there. Something very old. And very alive. The way the water rushed down the creek from the mountain. The smell of peat and hawthorn berries and sometimes snow filling the air.

But none of that came to me on that trip. Mostly I remember loving being with you. Loving that we both got to climb the mountain for the first time together, even though you lived less than 2 hours away your whole life. We listened to music the whole way there and the whole way back. It made me love the trip even more.

26

Skellig Michael

There is an island off the coast of County Kerry. It juts out of the ocean 8 miles from the mainland, an otherworldly-looking rock. It has been featured in two Star Wars movies to date, episode 7 The Last Jedi & episode 8 The Force Awakens.

It's called Skellig Michael or Sceilg Mhichíl in Irish. And in September 2015 I made it to her shores.

I've heard stories from the Irish and tourists alike – not everybody does make it to the island. It's a weather-dependent event, and even if the boat does go out, it's not guaranteed to land. If the sea is too rough, back you go. I know people who have tried 5 times and still haven't set foot there.

What I'm trying to say is this – we were lucky! My friend and I decided on a whim to give it a try. He made a call and suddenly we were booked for the next day to go. I love adventures like this. The kinds that excite you without too much time to doubt your decision.

I'd tell you the name of the boat company we took, but I cannot remember it. I can tell you we were booked with Casey's out of Portmagee, County Kerry. The morning of, as we waited for departure, my friend's name was called aloud. "Cian?" His name floated up out of the mouth of a crusty Irish fisherman. We both sat upright.

Turns out there was a delay of 30 minutes with our booking, and we had the chance to jump on another boat and leave right away. Cian looked at me as if to say, what do you think, should we risk it? Cian was always assessing risk.

I nodded and up we got and over we went onto another boat. And to this day I have no idea who we travelled with. I also remember that there were no life jackets to be seen. None were ever offered and honestly, I didn't see any place where they could have been stored.

St. Finian's Bay spilled out into the open ocean and as our little, teeny-tiny, no life jacket boat drove past sun-drenched hills and colourful houses, everyone was quiet, looking ahead for our first glimpse of the rock. I held onto the railing, enjoying the feel of our boat's movements on the water. My friend held onto the side in a slight slump, anticipating his seasickness.

Once we left the protected bay, the swells began. Forward and backward, then side to side; it was like riding a horse! For the first twenty minutes, I revelled in the movement. I held onto the railing, face full of smile, and rocked with the motion. I felt like a kid.

And slowly a pointy dark thing began to emerge and became larger until it became clear, and it was the island itself, like a giant tooth emerging from the water.

I could feel the beginning of that strange sleepiness that seems to accompany sea sickness come over me when we were about halfway out. And as my own downward spiral began, I felt like that tooth couldn't come fast enough! I was just barely holding it together. My friend on the other hand was not so lucky. He was retching over the side, the sound completely drowned out by the wind. It's a strange thing to see someone so violently ill, but unable to hear a sound. I wanted to comfort him. But there is no comfort for the seasick.

I was as white as a sheet when the boat pulled up to the dock. Thank God! If we'd had to turn around, I don't think I would have made it. My friend later told me he was prepared to jump overboard and swim to the landing spot should the boat decide landing wasn't an option. I believe his exact words were, "Fuck that!".

We climbed out, all wobbly, and walked up the path to a rock to sit down. Then we laid down. All I could see were blue skies, some white, almost see-through strips of clouds, and the occasional gull. It was so beautiful. Slowly our sea legs were replaced with stone and earth legs, and the queasiness died down and we felt well enough to continue up the exposed hillsides of Skellig Michael.

From April to July, sometimes into August, the island becomes a breeding colony for the Atlantic puffin. Normally a sea bird, spending their winters in the open ocean of the North Atlantic and Arctic, they come ashore to lay their eggs in rabbit burrows and grow their chicks or pufflings as baby puffins are called!

Unfortunately, we missed the puffins. But Cian told me he had been once before with an American friend of his and the island had been absolutely covered with these noisy birds, their black and white feathers an homage to the penguin, their multi-coloured beaks reminiscent of the toucan.

We finished climbing the roughly 670 stone steps that led up to the beehive huts of the monastery, whose creation by former monks is thought to have begun in the 6th century. Sometime in the 10th century, it was dedicated to St Michael, the Archangel Protector, and Skellig Michael became a sought-after position for many monks. In fact, there was even a waitlist to get on the island! The 8-mile journey in a currach did not deter them. Currachs, by the way, are wooden boats with animal hides stretched over them, using oars or sails for movement. Can you imagine?

By the time we reached the top, the weather had cleared. The day had begun quite grey and was shifting back and forth between sun and mood up until this point. As the clouds disappeared, Little Skellig became visible, about 1.5km from where we stood. Another rocky tooth rising. Flecks of white showing its true purpose, a bird colony, now filling our eyes.

Long ago, these two islands were one – a mountain range that was uplifted around 300 million years ago. They say that the red sandstone that makes up these rocks was pushed North a few centimetres a year from warm, equatorial seas. And through erosion and rising sea levels, the two peaks of Great and Little Skellig had become islands.

As our tour guide spoke, Irish accent thick and beautiful, I could see Cian in his red coat, hat covering his head to keep him warm. His seasickness had dissipated, and he looked a normal colour, tan and brown from his daily encounters with the elements. I smiled. I was so happy we'd made it on shore and taken the time out of our work schedules to be there. I remembered the moment he asked me if I wanted to go, and my yes was an all-in kind of yes. But that meant finding a way to get out of work. Andrew, if you're reading this now, apologies!

I feigned sickness the day of, calling from the Quill's parking lot in Glengarriff and praying no one I knew saw me. West Cork is so tiny, it would be easy for word to somehow travel that I had been seen, and my fake excuse discovered. I reclined the seat in my car as far down as it would go and waited for Cian to pick me up. No one saw us!

But our luck did not continue.

On Skellig Michael itself, we met a woman who worked at the nature reserve in Glengarriff and knew both of us. See, told you, Ireland is small! But in the end, my lie was not uncovered, and I lived a beautiful day on an ancient island instead of making coffee for tourists and cutting cheese. Priorities!

On our way back to Portmagee, our captain announced that he was dropping us back on the mainland only to return and collect the leftover gear from the most recent Star Wars filming instalment, The Last Jedi. They had just wrapped up a week ago. Now all those boxes and bags tucked to the side near a small building by the landing dock made sense. As did all the Puffin Wars t-shirts I'd seen on the mainland before departure.

The waves rocked us as we travelled back, passing Little Skellig to get a glimpse (and smell) of the gannet sanctuary. They say there are about 35,000 breeding pairs of gannets on this rocky outcrop. The largest numbers in Ireland and one of the largest in the world. The wind and the boat's motor dimmed the sounds of these large and noisy seabirds, their rolling grating calls barely cutting through.

Cian held onto the railing. I can't remember what I did. All I know is we made it back safely, without any life jackets. Without any regrets. And a photo of me holding a giant wooden hammer that belonged to one of the island's caretakers, who stood next to me in the photo. He used it to keep the stone steps in place. And only occasionally, when they were very rowdy, would he use it to keep tourists who didn't obey the rules in their place. Or so he said.

One of the most beautiful things about Ireland, and about this day in general, was the shifting light. The grey, overcast skies breaking up and eventually bringing white clouds and blue holes and then finally completely clearing, the bright sun shining on all things. Each of these moments and their transitions bring unique colours to the sea. Colours like deep blue, blue-grey, and milky green. Watching the ever-shifting light that day was incredible.

27

The Bardic School

The Sheep's Head Peninsula is full of wonders. Wild goat herds, hidden coves and piers, carnivorous plants, and even a concrete bunker from World War II!

The wonders also reach further back into time. There are holy wells – old water sources of religious or spiritual devotion. The locals say one should never speak on the journey to one of these wells – it undoes the power held there. Only after you leave may you talk.

There are the remains of ringforts, once built as protection for the Neolithic Irish people. There's even a 15th – 16th-century castle ruin called Rossmore that overlooks Dunmanus Bay.

But one of my favourite places, both personally and from the stories it holds, are the ruins of a Medieval Bardic School near Lake Farranamanagh outside the village of Kilcrohane.

The ruins of this ancient place sit atop a hill with wide sweeping views of the bay and the Mizen peninsula across it. I always got a sense of peace as I wandered down the trail there, stopping amidst the ruins, wondering what life must have been like in the 13th century.

I mean, a Bardic School in this place was truly at the ass end of nowhere in mediaeval times. Yet, it had ties to the Spanish throne and many famous filídh, the Irish word for Poets, graduated from its stone dwellings.

To call it a Bardic School may be somewhat of a misnomer. Bards were part of the entourage of a Poet. They gave voice to their creations. But the Poets themselves? They were men and sometimes women who became not only history keepers, but lawgivers and mystics. Early Irish law or Brehon law considered Poets true nobles, and they had a lot of influence in Irish society.

To say the schooling of a Poet was intense would be an understatement. The process of becoming one took 7 to 12 years, and their studies included learning 300 poetic metres, 250 primary stories, and 100 secondary stories. They had to master and commit to memory genealogies, learn prophecy, the skill of praising rulers (whom their livelihoods depended on), and so much more. If you were to look at their mediaeval syllabus it would take your breath away and include other subjects such as Irish history, Brehon law, language, and literature. These people were highly educated and truly skilled.

At school, they worked alone in their bedrooms, which often consisted of no more than stone cells with very little natural light or a few candles. They'd work in darkness, creating their pieces and then bring them out into the light of day to perform for their master and receive feedback.

The school year ran from September 29th through to March 25th, the wettest and darkest parts of the year. And once school was out, they'd wander the country, being given hospitality no matter where they went. It was the law. No one could turn away a Poet.

Nowadays, the trail descends boggy ground from the Bardic College ruins above, along the sea, and then back inland to Farranamanagh Lake. The beautiful brackish waters are surrounded by reeds, with swans paddling its surface.

One of the old stories of this place says that those swans are inhabited by the spirits of two Spanish princes. Long ago, a Spanish King sent his sons to study at the Bardic College. They drowned in the lake, turned into swans, and can be found, to this day, on its ever-shifting surface.

To stand at the shores of this lake now, it's hard to believe the fame of the Irish Poets who came from this place. The peninsula used to be known as The Rhymer's Peninsula, its reputation reaching far and wide beyond the shores of West Cork and Ireland herself all the way to Elizabethan England and beyond.

Shakespeare actually wrote about them in *As You Like It*. The comedy's main character, Rosalind, was banished by her uncle the Duke. She runs away, dressing up as a boy, and says this famous line referring to the Poets:

"I was never so berhymed since Pythagoras' time that I was an Irish rat, which I can hardly remember."

What in the world does that mean, you might be wondering? People who followed the teachings of Pythagoras believed in reincarnation and the Irish were known to rhyme rodents to death—she's inferring that she could have been one of those unlucky rats in a previous life.

There are stories from Mediaeval times saying that the Irish Poet's tongue was so witty, so sharp, and so powerful that not only could they banish and kill rats, they could do the same to a human. In Brehon Law, a Poet could be sentenced to death for murder in this way.

Modern day Ireland has seen both these laws and the Rhymer's who once wielded their words like weapons shapeshift or vanish altogether. The one thing that hasn't changed though? The wit. It can still sucker punch you if you aren't ready for it.

There's so much we can learn from the research that's been done to help us understand what life was like for these Poets and Irish society at the time, but even so, there are many mysteries that remain.

Like the connection between the Bardic School and Drombeg Stone Circle. Drombeg is dated between 153BC and 127AD. The Bardic School was built in an almost straight line hundreds of years later, about 24.5 miles as the crow flies, from Drombeg.

Or the missing stone slab from the Bardic School. John Tobin, a Sheepshead resident, tells the story, recounted to him by his sister Jo Jo. Back in the 1950s a stone slab was discovered in a building being used as a hen house on the site of the ruins. John's father Dick didn't recognise the language of the writing on the slab, but he knew it wasn't English or Irish. The Irish Folklore Commission was notified of the find and the intention was to preserve the building and record the artefact. Unfortunately, this process took a long time and when someone finally made it to the property, the stone slab had gone missing. To this day, it hasn't been found. What could it teach us about the Bardic school and all that transpired on a lonely finger of land called the Sheep's Head Peninsula?

I spent a lot of time exploring around there. Always drawn to this spot. I was brought by friends for walks and brought my friends to walk there in turn. The views, the mysteries, and the backdrop of the Bardic School ruins a constant, along with the wind. It's a beautiful and magical spot, imbued with the spirit of creativity. Maybe that's why I kept coming back, being a creative myself? Maybe that's why I felt called to sing out to the sea, the sheep, the hay bales, and the bogs of this place?

A place tied to Poets.

28

Swimming in Light

We got naked and climbed down the cold, concrete steps in the dark, laughing with excitement.

I was already anticipating the cold water, half holding my breath and bracing myself for the shock of iciness that I'd now come to equate with Irish waters.

My friend Rosalee walked behind me – two Americans on a remote pier at the end of the earth. How did we get here?? I mean, I know how we got here! But sometimes if you just sit and ponder the series of choices that led you to the very moment you're in, it's wild. And kind of beautiful.

Diving into bioluminescent water is like a child's imagination come to life. Tiny sparks of light ripple out all around you as you pave a path through the salt and waves. It's easier to see from above or beside, but it's magic no matter where you position yourself.

Rosalee and I slide ourselves in and watched the sparks fly. The saltwater felt amazing on our skin with nothing between us and it. It all felt so soft, silky and smooth. The night was thick with darkness and a gentle breeze blew, though we were in a protected part of Dunmanus Bay, cliffs half circling us as we swam.

Little moments like these filled my time in Ireland. Little moments full of life where my senses drank in more than my mind. Little moments that could easily be forgotten. They filled my life there, but really, they fill all of our lives. With pleasure and wonder and a little bit of ache.

I remember this time I was at the Bantry market, not long after I'd moved overseas. I was speaking with a woman who was telling me a story about a sailor she loved and all the adventures he'd been on in his long life. This was the stuff of movies! And I thought, you know, this man's story will never be known by the wide world. It will never be commercialised. And there was something about that that I loved. You see, we are the people who have the stories, and they are ours to tell. The disconnect between popular media and the human experience is very real and I see that gap widening with social media and online life exploding. I think it's something we need to take care with. And I think we always need to remember that each of us, in our way, has a story to share. Whether it's something simple like swimming in bioluminescent water with an old friend or something sexier, like seeing Jimi Hendrix perform in Clonakilty, West Cork in the 1970s.

I don't know though. We *were* two naked redheads swimming in the sea. What's sexier than that?

Acculturated

" The Irish are the one race for whom psychoanalysis is of no use whatsoever. "

-From the movie *The Departed*, attributed to Sigmund Freud

The funny thing about Ireland is that most of its residents speak English as their primary language, but the culture of Ireland is night to America's day. We are all speaking the same language, but we are most definitely saying something completely different. From the word homely to the word fuck, from the multi-layered empathy to the mindsets of Irish people, these stories capture some of the unique culture of this small island and how I lost and found myself again inside of it.

29

Homely Candles and Other Weird Words

When the phrase left his moustached mouth, I froze. Did he really just say that?

I could feel my brain searching for file cards inside the museum of my mind for reference. Nada. Nothing. I was searching for something beyond the literal because he couldn't possibly mean that literally?

"Yeah, then we can just fuck him in the back!"

He was telling me a story about a guy he didn't like. We started joking about how we would handle it, running into him. He began word weaving, about seeing him on the side of the road while we drove, stopping his van, and that we could grab him and just fuck him in the back.

The Irish have an amazing vocabulary and grasp of the usage of expletives. They use them quite frequently, more so than Americans, which totally surprised me! I was once on Bus Eireann in Cork City, fresh off the plane with a jet-lagged soul (and eyes) when two Irish, grey-haired men began conversing behind me. Every other word was fuck. Breaking the stereotype of grandads, these guys could have beaten a ship full of sailors in a swearing contest. I turned around in surprise, with a modicum of delight. Was this really happening?

Turns out fuck is used in ways I didn't even know were possible in Ireland. For instance, fuck him in the back means, throw him in the back. It's a verb! Here's another example of how to use this form of fuck:

"Do you want any more water?"

"No, you can just fuck it in the back!!!"

When my friend explained what he meant, I died laughing. And started using this new form of fuck immediately.

I had another language shock in a candle store once.

My friend Bernie and I were in Dingle town on the Dingle Peninsula for a mini girl's getaway. We walked the streets exploring the tiny shops and pubs, restaurants, and hotels when we decided to enter a store full of candles. It was a chilly day, so the light and smell drew us in like two moths to a flame.

I wandered around with pleasure eyes taking in the fragrances, things like bergamot, grapefruit, and tobacco when a sign caught my eye.

Homely Candles

I looked around for a dictionary.

Surely they meant Homey Candles? In the United States homely means unattractive or plain in appearance. While Homey means cozy, comfy, of the home.

Nope ... they meant Homely.

Turns out that in Ireland, the UK and even South Africa homely means simple, cosy, and comfortable. Notice the 's' in cosy this time? Another difference between Ireland and the US. Z's are replaced with S's.

I was beginning to realise that while we were all speaking English in this country, we were indeed speaking different languages.

Then there was the time I walked into the community hall in Caheragh wearing one of my favourite t-shirts – Shift Happens.

It always got a lot of attention. I'd discovered that the computer nerds in Seattle loved it, the yogis too. Once I was walking into my therapist's office with it on. I saw her door open, and a man walked out, so I began to walk toward him to enter her room. I'll never forget it. Almost as if in slow motion we stared at each other as we walked past, him taking in my shirt and me, his. His said "Shit Happens".

Now imagine my surprise when I discovered shift had another meaning!

As we made our way through the different ceilidh dancing sets that night in Caheragh I navigated stares. I was starting to become a little self-conscious. Did everyone think it said Shit Happens? Because that happened a lot! I couldn't figure it out.

Luckily Liam, the light-footed organiser pulled me aside to ask how the dance was going and informed me that, in Ireland, "shift" means a good make-out session.

Later on, I'd discover my friends, especially those in the dating pool, would use the word. For instance, "Ah, I had a great shift outside the pub last night." Yep, shift does indeed happen.

Of course, there are many other language discrepancies:

Aubergine for eggplant

Coriander for fresh cilantro

Jumper for sweater

Lorry for truck

And beautiful, almost poetic phrases to describe daily events, like:

The sun is nearly ripening me now (It's hot!)

or

She winds me up like a clock (She pisses me off!)

Piss or Pissed is another difference. In the US pissed means angry, while in Ireland it generally means being absolutely wasted drunk.

One other little word almost got me into a heap of trouble. And it will probably surprise you.

Ride. In the States, if you want someone to take you somewhere in their car you'd say, can I have a ride?

In Ireland, ride is overtly sexual and means, essentially, can I have a ride...on you!

I've loved languages for as long as I can remember. I used to spend hours as a child reading, sometimes staying up super late to finish a Lucy Maud Montgomery novel or a creepy R.L. Stine Goosebumps story. When my cousin and I would get together we'd read everywhere. In treehouses, in bed, on the beach during vacations – we were never without a book.

As an adult, I read much less. (My cousin on the other hand still takes a book with her everywhere she goes.) But the delight is still there. Whenever I hear a new word or phrase, either in English or another language, it causes me to pause and drink it in. My (and our) human experiences are so varied, it feels good to have options to describe them. Ireland consistently scrambled my brain and surprised me in this way.

'Safe Home.'

'What's the craic?'

'I'm after eating.'

and the use of the word ye for we.

30

The Power of the Thumb

The only place I've ever hitchhiked is in Ireland and I can't remember what gave me the courage to try.

I think it was a mix of desire, hearing stories that it's a relatively safe country, and feeling somewhat at home, like I belonged there. I never had a proper scary experience – though I did have a few curious ones!

The first time I ever hitched was a 33 km journey from Baltimore to Schull. As the crow flies it's only about 13 km, but the waters of Roaringwater Bay cut inland like puzzle pieces so the journey takes much longer by land.

I remember I was taking the ferry from Sherkin Island back to the mainland when I decided I was finally going to go for it. I was going to hitchhike. As the ferry cut through choppy waters heading towards shore and I gathered my courage, I heard two men speaking a mysterious language. The sounds intrigued me and helped take my mind off the fear that was upon me. I couldn't place it, but my ears and mind were leaning towards something Eastern European. Finally, I relaxed and opened my ears, kind of like what you do with those magic eye photos – where you go into wide-angle vision and the image finally pops out of what seems like a sea of colour? And I discovered that they weren't speaking Latvian or Polish, but plain and simple English with thick-as-mud Irish accents. Once I heard it, I couldn't unhear it.

I stepped onto the pier and walked uphill to the edge of the village. I'd heard that you needed to choose your hitch point carefully, making sure the driver had enough time to see you and decide what they wanted to do and then have plenty of room to pull safely off the road.

I stuck my thumb out and waited. God, my thumb looked weird! I hadn't noticed it's strange, double-jointed shape in a while. I stared at it in weird awe and then finally shifted my gaze toward town, the grey sky, and moving clouds.

Ten minutes felt like an hour. Car after car passed me. Some of them did this little hand motion that I'd later learn meant they were driving just down the road, somewhere nearby and it wouldn't be worth it for me if they stopped. Some gave me the one or two-finger salute, a classic West Cork greeting. But it was the wood-panelled van that finally stopped. As the sliding back door opened a puff of smoke escaped and inside was a French couple on their way to Schull, Ray Charles blasting from their sound system. They seemed friendly enough, so I threw my big red backpack in and had a seat. Turns out, while a little scattered, they were solid people. We stopped for paint in Skibbereen and then they let me out at the top of Schull town. Unscathed. Exhilarated. And on time.

My early hitches were either interesting or uneventful. But the guy from Cool Mountain in West Cork took it a step towards weird, like my thumb. I'd driven my mom up to the Cork airport in our rental car for her flight back to the States and decided I wanted to challenge myself and hitch all the way home. Normally the drive takes one and a half hours. And I'd hitched it in less than two. But this time I was not so lucky!

The space between my lifts was super long and some of the people who picked me up only took me short distances. So when, let's call him Tom, picked me up at the edge of Enniskean and said he'd take me all the way to Bantry, I was really excited.

He was young, dressed in sweatpants (which is pretty common amongst Irish lads), and seemed kind enough – no big alarm bells. I hopped into his coupe – it was old but clean, and we talked as he drove. Me being me, I started asking him a lot of questions. In retrospect, I think Tom thought I was being flirty. Little did he know I was just being myself!

Anyway, I found out he grew up on Cool Mountain, an old hippie commune settled in the 1970s by English immigrants trying to escape Margaret Thatcher's rule. These days it is infamous for its outdoor parties and drug use. Tom was a DJ and went on and on about music and how he wanted to build his own house, and I don't even know what else anymore. The kinds of things that young people say in their 20s when they haven't really done anything yet and are full of dreams that may or may not make it to reality.

As we got closer to Bantry, Tom was having such a good time that he offered to take me all the way to Ahakista to the house where I was staying. Grateful, as I'd been on the road for ages, I agreed. Didn't even occur to me that he might have had something else in mind!

We drove the winding road out of Durrus and the first sight of the Atlantic made me catch my breath, as it always did. On we went along the sea, through the village of Ahakista, and up a narrow winding road to my friend Sheila's house, where I was staying.

Tom pulled up her long gravel driveway, stopped by the house, and turned off his ignition. My car was in the driveway packed to the gills. I was getting ready to move later that day. As I began to gather my things and thank him, he spoke again.

"Can I come inside?" Tom said.

I stopped moving.

My brain was running around trying to decipher what he meant. I'd told him my friend Sheila had built her own house. Was that why?

I was silent.

Tom tried again.

"Can I come inside and get to know you better?"

Since that moment I have thought of like 10 different responses, all connected to a different vibe, but in the moment I played dumb. I laughed, mumbled some excuse and got out of the car.

Honestly, I felt a tiny bit unsafe. Would he leave? Would he come back later? This wasn't even my place; it was my friend's! Tom never returned. And I've gotten a lot of mileage out of that story. Cue the porn music, please...

Then there was the guy who asked me for my number. And another one who asked me out on a date. But this time he was hitchhiking! I picked him up outside of Glengarriff near the Eccles Hotel. He was an older looking 21 and guessed immediately that I was from the US. It was my gum chewing that gave me away, he said. I gave him my number cause he was kinda cute but decided against it in the end.

One of the cool things about hitching in West Cork is that sometimes people you know pick you up, which is almost always a relief. Unless you run into one of the odd ducks. And there are a good few odd ducks in West Cork! Like creepy spiritual guys, or bachelor farmers who just don't have normal social skills or someone I actually knew who took the conversation from 'How are you finding Ireland' to anal sex. Do not even ask how that happened! Two weeks after picking me up he actually passed away suddenly. So, to honour the departed he shall remain nameless, and the rest of that conversation will live in the archive halls of my mind.

One day a woman picked me up. She told me that whenever she saw a hitchhiker she always tried to stop. She'd hitchhiked a lot in her early years and wanted to pay it forward. I'd come to find out this was quite common. Before the 90s very few people in Ireland had cars. And, like bus stops, there were hitching spots where you needed to stand in line until it was your turn.

Then there was the day Michael Jackson died. I was hitching from a rural area into the local village when a son and his elderly mother stopped and gave me a lift. Not a ride mind you. A ride is something completely different in Ireland (see previous story).

The radio announcer came on to let all of us know that Mr. Jackson died of cardiac arrest in Los Angeles. The details were vague at the time, but the case was eventually deemed a homicide, a combination of sedatives and propofol had stopped his heart.

We started chatting about his music and to my great surprise, this 80+ year old woman said she really enjoyed it.

"He had that one song. What is called? What was it called Tadgh? Ah, yes! Bad. I loved that one."

I wanted to laugh out loud with pleasure at the words that had come out of this Irish granny's mouth. People can be very surprising. And I love to be surprised.

If you don't have a car, hitchhiking in Ireland gives you the freedom to see places that buses don't go. And the bus system doesn't go to *a lot* of places in Ireland. I've also done it for one-way hikes. I once walked the old road from Killarney into Kenmare. I drove up over the Caha Pass into Kenmare town, parked near the edge of the village, and put my thumb out. It was a Sunday morning. 9 am. There was barely a soul. Imagine my surprise when a Dutch tour bus pulled over and welcomed me in. The driver was charismatic, asked me my story, and then translated it into Dutch for his guests. At a coffee stop that involved biscuits an elderly gentleman asked if I was single and took his picture with me, and then they dropped me off at my hike entry point. It really made my day.

If you ever decide to try hitchhiking, here are a few tips:

1. Trust your gut. If you get a weird vibe, don't get in.

2. As I said at the beginning of the story, find a good spot. Make sure drivers have plenty of time to see you and a safe place to pull over.

3. Make sure to have the conversation about where they're going and where you're hoping to be and weigh up whether it's a good fit. You don't have to get in.

4. Be kind. Wear your seatbelt. And be friendly. You might make a friend for life. Or hear an interesting story.

5. Say thank you. How amazing is it, that in a world full of so much tragedy, we can still rely on the kindness of strangers?

6. Reminder of the hand signs:

+ A quick point down the road ahead? This means they're local and probably aren't going far enough to warrant a stop for you. But they want you to know they aren't ignoring you. Because they're kind. And Irish.

+ One or two fingers raised? They're saying hello! It's the Cork or Kerry Salute. This means they don't have to take their hand off the steering wheel, but can still greet ya. And they won't be picking you up.

+ Giving you the middle finger? Lol. Just kidding. But if they did? Definitely don't get in.

31

Set Dancing in Ballylickey

There's a pub in West Cork called the Ouvane Falls Inn.

It sits near a crossroads with signs pointing to Bantry and Cork and Glengarriff. Behind the old building, a rushing waterfall stemming from the Owvane River flows into the salty waters of Bantry Bay. Set in the townland of Ballylickey, it's a beautiful spot.

On Tuesday nights a group of set dancers meet to practise their céilí dancing there. It's a local's local spot with occasional outsiders such as myself or people volunteering on farms in the area showing up for a pint and some dancing.

Céilí, pronounced Kay-*lee*, is an old form of folk dancing that originates in Ireland and essentially means 'a social visit'. It's a kind of group dancing where couples form a set of four and dance different patterns through a set of songs. One of my favourites, the Borlin Set, is named after a gorgeous valley up the road and up a mountain from the Ouvane Falls. It's a bouncy polka with 5 different sets of dances that are really fun. They make you breathless!

I'm not gonna lie, sometimes listening to Irish céilí music and Irish Trad music in general, does my head in after about an hour. It's like binge-watching three seasons of Derry Girls – why are they always yelling at each other?? The nature of the music is repetitive, I think that's what it is. But hearing it live and dancing to it makes me happy. There's usually a diverse range of ages at local dances too. One time I even danced with my immigration officer: Hi Mairead!

One cold and dark Tuesday night I showed up to dance at the Ouvane. It was busy! Most of the dancers were over 50, lived in the area, and had probably known each other for their entire lives. I, on the other hand, stood out like a sore thumb. Well, me and this French woman. We were in sets next to each other and I could feel the difference, between myself and her as one group and everyone else. But I couldn't place why at first.

Our instructor began the evening with announcements and stories and that's when it hit me. I watched as the crowd respond to his words. It felt like a ripple would move through the Irish people, like they were interconnected and responding more as a group than as individuals. Like when you watch a flock of birds moving together, in sync, shifting direction with ease yet staying close to one another. It was like that. Like ripples of connection. And the French woman and me? We seemed more like individuals. Clearer in our place as ourselves.

This was often my experience in Ireland. Irish people are very attuned to 'other'. Sometimes at their own expense. I watched friends of mine struggle with their mental health whenever they decided to do something out of the norm. Like, hang out alone or with one other person instead of a big group. Or create a new offering. Out of the norm always brought questions, judgments, and a lot of gossip in some of these small coastal villages.

But the bright side? Irish people respond to who you are and how you are being. They have keen intuition. They know how to take care of someone and are understanding, kind and generous people.

I think the Irish have good medicine for Americans. And that loops around to return the favour. A healthy sense of community mixed with a healthy sense of self increases our likelihood of true belonging, not at the expense of ourselves, but because we are ourselves within a group.

Brené Brown talks about this in her book *Braving the Wilderness*. And Bill Plotkin in his book *Nature and the Human Soul*. It's a genuine need, to belong and to be yourself. One without the other is a life half-lived. A shell. Or a rebellion.

Anyway, back to set dancing! We danced a lot that night. Sweat a lot. And laughed a lot. We danced the Connemara Set, the Ballyvourney Jig, and the Antrim Square. I drank a pint of the cold and dark Murphy's Stout in between dances and sat down and chatted with everyone. But that ripple of connection at the beginning? That was what struck me the most. I've been thinking about it ever since.

32

People of the Wild Atlantic Way

Have you ever been to a portrait exhibition?

It is the most intimate thing, looking at a large photograph of a human being. The eyes are so big. It just feels so personal, somehow even more so than looking at someone right in front of you. Maybe it's because you can really stare and take in all their glimmers and lines and pops of personality. And no one cares cause its art and you're allowed to look.

The first one I ever attended was in Bantry, showcasing stunning 1 metre by 1 metre black and white photographs of musicians, artists, and various local figures. Little did anyone know – my own portrait was also among them!

That is, until one of my friends, or one of their siblings or sometimes even friends of friends would wander into town and happen upon me looking down at them. It happened to one of my friends in the Brick Oven. And later to another when they went in to do some banking at AIB. Somehow, I always seemed to be above them looking down. It's nothing personal, just had to do with the hanging height.

So how did I end up on the walls of the local businesses in Bantry? Me, an American, spending a few years living abroad? It's simple really. When Bernie O Sullivan phones you up one day and asks you if you want to be a part of an artist's project and you're into that kind of thing you say yes. The rest is history.

People of the Wild Atlantic Way was a concept created by Dublin-born photographer Shay Hunston. He wanted to capture the essence of the Irish. To him that meant highlighting their warmth and friendliness. It's the thing that most travellers to Ireland notice and what touches them during their time there. I know that was true for me.

The Wild Atlantic Way was a tourism initiative that launched in 2015, the year I moved over. Its job was and still is to highlight the natural beauty around Ireland's coastline along with the history, people, and stories of place. The hope was that this would draw in tourists, in a sustainable way – a way that benefitted both people and nature.

So in June 2016 when Shay started his project documenting Ireland's people, the Wild Atlantic Way was just getting started and made for a nice pairing! His goal is to make it from Kinsale to Donegal. As of today, he's still winding his way.

"The project is a celebration of these wonderful people living on the west coast of Ireland, an open-minded, independent, welcoming, tolerant people – people free in spirit and wild at heart, living on the edge of the world," Shay said in an interview with Go Wild Magazine.

For each portrait taken, Shay also did a brief interview with the person and asked them life or craft related questions, then took snippets from the interview and included them with the portrait upon exhibition.

Here's mine:

'If I had to give advice to my younger self, I would have said, really learn to listen, that would have made music way easier to learn. When you learn to listen, you realise that there is a lot in the spaces, you are not trying to stuff them full, it can become exhausting always trying to fill the space with something.

When I do that, it opens up an entirely new world and I feel relaxed and open to the moment, ideas come in and I can follow them more easily, I also become inspired by the musicians I'm playing with.

Another thing I would have told myself is, never apologise for love, sometimes it can get messy or maybe there are some things that need apologising for, but never apologise for loving someone.

As a singer, the more I open up to my emotions and feelings, the more my body resonates and the more interesting my music becomes. I become free, instead of performing, I am living the music.'

I remember the day he photographed me. I was so nervous. I took a shower the morning of and then immediately regretted it. My hair is a mane and I thought the mane would have looked beautiful, but washing it tamed and straightened my curls, making it look a little limp. So I was going into Bantry's old movie cinema with some insecurities.

I remember Shay asked me to smile broadly and then close my mouth, keeping the smile alive in my eyes. Like the Mona Lisa in the Louvre in Paris. I remember it was a sunny day. And Bernie came with me. I remember being glad she was there.

When it was over I left the darkness of the building and walked out into the sunshine, full of delight and relief. It would take months for the Bantry exhibition to get underway and for me to start receiving those random texts from people who'd just discovered my photo here or running into people who'd just discovered my photo there when they were running errands around town.

I feel honoured to have been included in this massive undertaking. And whenever I re-encounter the photographs I can feel my eyes begin to tear up and my heart open. People's souls are easy to see in this medium. And the beautiful smile wrinkles around their eyes share so much more than just their words ever could.

33

Irish Empathy

I once heard the comedian Trevor Noah do a piece on travelling in England and how much he enjoyed the people there.

He joked about the empathy of the English and how they're so concerned for the feeling they think you might be feeling. When he said this, I burst out laughing! That was 100% my experience of the Irish.

I remember when I first landed in West Cork. I began to meet people and form friendships, and I definitely noticed this kind of empathy. Something else began to happen too. It's something called mirroring. And it was naturally occurring between myself and my new acquaintances.

One night a friend of mine and I were out for dinner and talked the entire night, we were enjoying each other so much. That's when I began to notice that he was mirroring me. I'd change my body position and he'd follow me. It was all unconscious on his part. But I really noticed it!

I'd read about this kind of thing happening. When two people sync up they begin to mirror and mimic each other. That it's a natural process having to do with our deepest survival instincts, what we like, and maybe even who we're trying to influence.

I'd lean forward and put my elbows on the table, telling him about the time I gigged at the Triple Door in Seattle, and I'd notice him leaning forward as well, elbows down, the smell of him wafting over the dinner table. Then, just to test if it was real, I'd lean back against the chair and take a deep breath and there he'd be, leaning back himself, doing the same.

After multiple experiences of mirroring with different kinds of people I began to notice something else about Irish society. It's kind of complicated! In my experience there was regularly a big difference between what people said with their mouths and the actual vibe that was coming off their bodies – like two *very* different languages. It felt like you sometimes had to be a detective to discover what a person was actually meaning. That or incredibly intuitive. Because the truth is, most people likely won't tell you what's up. That would be too direct.

My mirroring friend and I were in a grocery store once after a movie, grabbing a few things. As we got in line at the checkout, I noticed the cashier had a weird vibe! Her body language was saying something completely different to her words and even her words didn't sync up or fully make sense. After the interaction I remember asking my friend, "Okay, so what really happened there? Because what she said and what she felt like were totally different and that was super confusing!" He laughed. For him, it was just another day in Ireland.

But that empathy and mirroring have their positive sides too. The Irish are some of the best hosts in the world. They are very good at anticipating your needs, making you feel welcome, and providing comfort. There is this relaxing easiness that they invite you into, one which many Americans don't experience at home. Except maybe in the South.

I remember there was a night I slept over at my friend Bernie's house. We were out at the pub and when we came home, she set me up in her spare room, then disappeared. 15 minutes later she came back with a hot water bottle to keep the chill off. We snuggled until the bed heated up with the combination of our bodies and the bottle and then off she went to her own pillow.

You never really feel alone in Ireland. People chat to you. Welcome you into their homes. Offer you a lift. Buy you a beer. It's just super common for people to give.

This beauty and kindness and "I'd give you the shirt off my back" kind of vibe does indeed have a shadowy side. It's been my experience that the Irish will sometimes offer you something that they don't feel good about giving, yet feel compelled to give. Complex social tallies pile up. People end up feeling used. And then they won't actually talk to you about it. Instead, they'll talk about you to other people. It ends up feeling twisted and you're unsure if you can trust anyone!

Here's a simple example that illustrates how complicated things can get.

Tea.

In the United States, if someone asks you for a cup of tea and you decline, that is the end of the story. If you end up wanting something, you ask. Or suffer. It's up to you. I'd say that's a good, general rule of thumb.

In Ireland, if someone asks you for a cup of tea, well, that is just a starting point! It normally goes something like this:

"Would ya like a cup of tea?"

"Oh no, I'm grand, thank you."

"Are ya sure? It's no trouble at all."

"Ah, no, no, no, I'm fine. Tanks very much."

Normal conversation resumes. Then five minutes later:

"Are ya sure you don't want a cuppa? I was gonna make one for myself anyway."

"Oh, well, sure, if you were gonna make one anyway..."

Sometimes it takes three offers before a person will say yes.

However, I've seen this method go completely awry.

Sometimes the person really doesn't want a cup of tea but then feels obliged because their host asked so many times. Sometimes the asker doesn't want tea at all but wants to make sure their guest feels comfortable. It becomes so murky. Who wants what?? We don't really know!

Honestly, there is something quite nice about this process too. It feels like a dance. Waltzing around manners and wants and needs and connection. It's not all bad. And if you take it with a grain of salt, it's not a big deal. The thing is, this kind of dance is regularly infused into so many different kinds of relationships and interactions that it becomes hard to trust the Irish. Do they even want what they say they do?

Navigating this part of empathy, especially as an American, was tough for me. At first, I tried it on, innocent-like, because travel teaches. And cultures beyond my own have so much knowledge and wisdom and creativity and I love learning firsthand. Then, I rebelled against the empathy – trying this whole empathy thing on leads to confusion!

But now I see it differently.

When you know what you want and *can* ask for it, this kind of social dance becomes poetry. You know you can stay safe, be real and still engage in a language that the person across from you understands. Sometimes you may choose not to buy in and walk your own road. And sometimes you may dance, because, why not!

34

How Small is Small?

It was a sunny day when we walked into the Sheep's Head Inn pub. I remember because once you walk inside the sun quickly disappears and you're met with cool temperatures, the natural light held at bay.

The light that did make it in was absorbed by the wooden interior. My friend Sheila and I sat at the bar for a drink and began chatting with the bartender, a strawberry-blonde woman called Sinead. Sheila seemed to know her and away they went talking about this person and that person. But soon, I became the topic of conversation.

"Hold on a minute," Sinead said and pulled her iPad out from underneath the bar. She stared at the screen for a couple of minutes. I wondered what she was doing and pulled a sip from my Murphy's.

Murphy's, the official stout of Cork County, began as an operation started by 4 brothers back in 1854. Once a true competitor to Guinness, they went bankrupt in 1982 and were taken over by Heineken. Still, it's good to order a Murphy's when you're in the county.

"Here it is!" Sinead said, breaking me out of my reverie. And there, in the dimly lit Sheep's Head Inn pub which is no longer open, Sinead pulled up a video of me singing.

I couldn't believe it.

"Yeah, someone sent this to me a few Sundays ago. They were at the gig you did with Kenny Dread in Schull and were like, you must check this new singer out! Come up to the pub!" Sinead recalled.

Schull is about 17 km from Durrus, with plenty of fresh air in between the villages. But still, small is small in Ireland, and small was having a video of my singing shared with me weeks after I sang, sent by someone I didn't know to someone else I didn't know.

I remember being struck by the kindness of it. And aware that it was likely true that this kindness could work the other way around, stories being spread about unpleasant moments just as easily. But I was new to small. New to being known, seen, watched, wondered about, and judged on the level of small Irish village small, so I smiled. How cool, I thought. How truly lovely. And it was.

As the years passed, I would come to discover many of the levels of smallness in West Cork.

Some of my friends struggled with it. They longed for anonymity and fewer questions about their life choices or creative projects.

Everyone always seemed to have something to say, and they didn't always say it to your face.

In my experience, the Irish are naturally curious people. I remember I had the loveliest conversation with a fisherman at the Baltimore Harbor on my first trip to Ireland. He asked me 101 questions about myself, my life, and what brought me to his shores. As we spoke, he reflected my choices back to me and encouraged me on my journey. He was present with me. I think that's what stood out. You could tell he was taking in the information I was sharing and letting it run through his own heart and mind to see what it struck inside.

That's the beautiful side.

The other side? Gossip.

You can feel it when it's gossip time. I distinctly remember running into an older-generation Irish woman that I knew locally. She asked me a series of rapid-fire questions, staring at me intently, closing the gap of space between us with alarming speed and literally noodling the information out of me and into her brain for social currency should she need it as she navigated her day.

But it wasn't just the women. Oh no. The men were equal in their ability to retain intense detail about the people in their lives. I'll never forget the moment it struck me. I was headed out hiking with a male friend of mine and a few of his mates. As we drove to Killarney to get to the trailhead these grown men erupted like a flock of hens. I can't remember the personal details they shared about the people in their circles, but I do remember being astounded by the stories they wove. The thought of keeping that much intimate information in my head about other people's lives made my brain want to break. Yes, these men could gossip as well as any woman.

As the years passed my impression of the Irish began to change. And I'd laugh as my Retreat to Ireland participants would come to me after an encounter with an Irish person. They'd always say the same kind of thing. "Wow, they were so nice! And so curious!"

Hmmmm ... curious? Or potentially just plain nosy?

I now understand that it's normal for people, of any gender orientation in West Cork, to talk to someone about someone else, exchanging information along with their own thoughts and feelings about the person or their situation. I found this disconcerting after a while and it's one of the reasons I eventually moved. But I let my retreat participants enjoy the cultural experience without my more seasoned take on the social dynamics of small.

I did draw the line with Peter, though.

Peter was trying to get in touch with a friend of mine. And my friend hadn't been responding. Let me be clear. I didn't know this man. I'd only heard stories here or there. I'd never met him before. And to be honest, I don't know *how* he knew who I was. But when we ran into each other he confirmed my identity and began asking how my friend was doing. A cascade of leading questions followed that made me feel uneasy. I could tell he was trying to figure something out through me, and it made my skin start to crawl.

I stopped him and brought out the 35 years of living in the United States that lived inside of me.

"Sounds like you should get in touch with him directly."

Now it was Peter's turn to squirm.

I remember leaving that social interaction a mix of upset, confused, and annoyed.

This happened more times than I can count with my own hands, with other people, and in other situations. After Round 29 of Irish Small versus Kat Koch, I finally had to have that Come to Jesus conversation with myself. It went something like this:

"Kat, look it, this is West Cork. This is what happens here. People talk about each other *all* the time. You literally cannot get away from it. It's embedded in the culture, has its positive sides, but if it really feels as yucky as you're sensing? Then I think you should seriously consider relocating."

As they say in South Africa, "Yasus!"

Yasus is another form of taking the Lord's name in vain. It comes out of people's mouths as an exclamation when something challenging is afoot. It's a relief to make that kind of sound instead of internalising something that just shouldn't be.

Then, there's *this* kind of the small.

The kind of small where you céilí dance with your immigration officer.

The kind of small where, even though you'd finally moved away and were just back for a visit, the postman (who knows you left) asks you how long you're home for.

It's the kind of small where, when your tire is flat and you don't have the tools you need, five different people help you and someone runs home to get the right tire iron.

And it's the kind of small where, when you hitchhike, people you know pick you up. Because they care.

It's still the kind of culture that thinks nothing of dropping by someone's home for a cup of tea unannounced. I personally love this ritual. I once tried it when I was back in the States. I was in my friend Rachael's neighbourhood in Seattle, so I drove to her apartment and rang her buzzer. She answered tentatively.

"Hey, Rachael! I was in the neighbourhood, so I thought I'd drop by."

"Kat?" she enquired, "Is that you?"

And while she let me in, she later requested I call her first if I was in the neighbourhood again.

Apparently, sometimes, small doesn't work in big cities.

I once asked a friend of mine how she dealt with the smallness. How did she handle all the stories and gossip and how sometimes you could get to know someone through stories told about them by lots of different people, without ever having met them?

Her reply was simple.

"You must decide for yourself what you think and how you feel. And know that others will feel differently."

I paused.

That made sense.

It also struck me. She was basically describing a level of tolerance to the polarity and tension of life. You make up your own mind and hold it within the greater context. From this place, a good deal of personal power wells up, like a spring. In my experience, the Irish are very 'us' or 'we' oriented. So, these two things combined, being group minded plus independent without making the group wrong, makes for a fascinating culture to be immersed in.

Sometimes when I imagine the social landscape of Ireland, it reminds me of a tangled ball of yarn. Or a large group of people surrounded by fog. What's real? How does this person really feel? Is this co-dependency? Interconnection? Both?

It feels like Rainbow Weather. Beautiful, colourful and full of illusion. One thing I sense for certain, the Irish are unique with a witty human psyche that has been shaped by ancient stories, religion, colonialism, and the never-ending rain that washes the land green through storms from the Atlantic Ocean.

So is that where small comes from?

35

Now you Enjoy That

The first time I heard the floating melodies of the traditional Irish song Inis Oírr (spelled Inisheer in English) was in a stark room in a community hall in Letterfrack, County Galway.

Played by a small group of local elementary school kids, the moment the first few notes came out of their instruments, I wanted to cry. A slow air, both simultaneously happy and sad, it's the kind of song that lets you know you're in Ireland.

I was in Letterfrack to assist a friend of a friend run a yearly festival called Bog Week. It's a community-oriented experience that highlights the natural wonders of the Connemara bog landscape, bringing experts into schools and hosting lively festivities like races and musical performances.

The next day at recess I asked one of the kids to teach me how to play the song on the small tin whistle I was travelling around with. And there, on the playground of a small village in the West of Ireland, my relationship with Inisheer began.

Inis Oírr is the smallest of the Aran Islands off the West Coast and visible from the Cliffs of Moher. Less than 3 km square in size and with only 260 permanent residents, its official language is Irish and the main draw for tourism is hiking.

I first stepped onto her shores to meet a weaver called Mairead.

It was Autumn and the slow drop of colour and leaf was abundant, though the island herself doesn't have many trees. Just lots of thick hedgerows and stone walls bordering roads and fields.

I was assisting an acquaintance on her Ireland Ethnobotany Exploration. With about 10 participants, it was a 2-week trip focused on nature, wildcrafting, and culture in north Kerry, Clare, and Connemara. And Mairead the weaver was a trip highlight!

Normally you can pop over to Inisheer from Doolin, the trip taking only 15 minutes. But the weather was so bad we had to go up the coast a ways and take a different, larger ferry across. I can't remember how long we were on that boat, but I do remember how incredibly seasick I became. Sitting crumpled up at the back of the boat, away from the rain, but still outside, I was left to my misery. Except for a kind ferry employee. She came by and handed me a sick bag. God, I needed it! She also brought water. I knew she had experience with this kind of thing, because she said very little, yet stayed with me as I tried to look for land. Land. Any land! It's really overwhelming when you're trying to orient yourself on the waves of seasickness and people try to connect with you, talk with you. It's the worst. Her quiet presence on the other hand was so comforting.

It took me a few hours on solid ground to come back into my body and senses. But one thing I will always remember about those early hours on the island was the bartender in one of the pubs. I walked in, red hair flowing, stomach finally settling, to order a drink. The man walked over and said something to me in a foreign language. My perplexed look flipped a switch in his brain, and he said, "Oh, sorry, what would you like?"

He'd spoken to me in Irish! By that time, I'd lived in Ireland two and a half years and while I'd been mistaken for a local, I'd never had someone speak Irish to me like it was the most natural thing. Irish is the primary language on Inis Oírr, so this felt like a gift.

The next morning, we walked to Mairead Sharry's home. She is an expert knitter, spinner, and weaver living and working on Inisheer. While not originally from the island, she married in and so began her love of fibres.

Mairead's house, with its low ceilings and classic wide Irish fireplace, was a cosy spot to begin our workshop. She brought out small looms and different coloured fibres and began to teach us how to make one of the traditional crios (or belt) patterns the island is known for. Working in pairs, everyone began their weaving journey, and I sat close by, taking photos and helping where needed. The peat fire smoked in the fireplace while Mairead moved like a hummingbird, here, there, and everywhere, helping each person as they wove their pattern.

After a couple of hours, our weaving focus waning, Mairead flitted into the kitchen and came back out to the fire. Hands moving deftly, I watched her take a lump of what looked like the beginning of bread in a cast iron pan and work it into a nice oval shape. She then placed the pan right onto the coals of the fire. As she made tea in the kitchen, I watched the bread begin to rise, take more shape, and brown. I can count the times I've seen people cook in this kind of old-fashioned way and I couldn't take my eyes off the bread – I was so curious as it puffed and cracked and began to give off a delicious smell.

"Right, it's time!" Mairead announced and one by one we came to her for our cup of tea and soda bread.

She had this way about her. The kind that automatically gives you some respect for her and makes you want to listen. And when it was my turn, she prepared my tea, looked me straight in the eye, and said, "Now you enjoy that." I swear, her eyes twinkled.

Her words struck me. Now you enjoy that. Hmmmm. Yes. Enjoyment. Taking pleasure. Letting the moment in. It was like I'd consulted an oracle for divine wisdom and this woman was giving it to me in tea and bread.

I stepped outside away from the smoke and chatter and put my enjoyments on the stone wall outside. I looked at the sea, the clouds, the green in the fields. I smelled my tea and took a sip. Ah, that's nice. And I actually took a break. Savouring the moments. The delicious warmth of the crusty bread. Just enjoying.

And then back we went. To learning and weaving until our time with Mairead in her cottage ended and we took the long walk back to our hotel.

I often think of that moment. It may have been the first time I consciously recognised another human telling me to enjoy my life. It's not a message we always receive, especially in the US. The messaging is so different. Modern life gets so busy sometimes, it's easy to get on the treadmill and forget you have a name, let alone a soul.

Now you enjoy that.

I've since been reminded of these words by other beautiful people in my life. And the lesson has expanded. Enjoy, open up, and trust most recently came to me, and this has helped me blossom in new and unexpected ways. But let's be raw and real for a moment – life can be really tough sometimes. It can suck. More for some than others. But continuing to find ways to come back to enjoyment feels like a life skeleton key that is worth holding onto.

Once the pain passes and is processed, coming back to enjoyment, openness, and trust seems like a great way to continue to engage with and co-create our lives. Otherwise, we are just desperately trying not to get hurt. And as life would have it, that just isn't possible. From broken bones to broken hearts, none of us are getting out of here alive.

Thanks, Mairead. What you said mattered to me. Changed me. I'm grateful for your wisdom. I love that it came with something so simple – tea, bread and a twinkle. I hope you are well.

36

I Almost Got Arrested

I was sitting at a beautiful table in a tent in the Maasai Mara when I got a text from my landlady, in Ireland.

Here's what it said: *Hi Kat. Hope you are ok and having a lovely time. I received a call from a guard in Glengarriff. He asks if you can call him on 085 8*** 86*. He said it's not serious. Take care of yourself and safe travels.*

In case you didn't know, a guard is a police officer. Yes, that's right, a cop was looking for me!

The joy from hours on a safari vehicle drained from my face. What in the world? It's a disconcerting thing to be worlds away in a foreign country from your home in another foreign country to discover that an officer of the law wants you to get in touch with him. I started to wonder if something was wrong with my visa and worry began to trickle in raindrops, but then I decided something. There was absolutely nothing I could do about it now. I was in Kenya learning about giraffe family structures and trying to find leopards – there was no time for Irish cops. That would simply have to wait.

That night, as I fell asleep, I saw the animals from the Mara in my mind's eye – cheetah, topi, lion, hyena – they played like a movie reel in my mind, the perfect bedtime story. And the memory of that text from Kate drifted off with them into the African night.

One week later I returned to Ireland. I didn't have any trouble getting into the country. I took that as a positive sign. I spent a couple of days in Dublin where I met a guy I was just starting to see at the time. I'd travelled so much and so far that the thought of getting on another form of public transit was like a violation. In the back of my mind, I remembered the Irish cop, but I was in no rush. Ireland had begun to rub off on me and what normally would have triggered me into action was put on the backburner for very important activities such as sleeping, Christmas shopping, and getting a drink with Mike.

Eventually, I took the bus down to West Cork, stone-walled fields and sheep passing by as I listened to music and remembered the amazing feeling of happiness I got when I walked off the plane for the first time in Nairobi. Then, finally, I was home. My stone cottage just where I'd left it.

After a long sleep, I began to unpack – my checkered Maasai blanket of red and blue, the hand drill kit two Maasai men had gifted me after we had a chat about the college football team from my hometown in the States, and the little gifts I'd gotten for friends and family. I began to settle back into my life at home, my next trip just a few weeks on the horizon.

Winter Solstice arrived, and I sensed it was time I drive down to the Gardai station in Glengarriff Village – I was finally ready to discover the truth about that mysterious message. I kept my eyes peeled for the colour of pink roses and finally found the station, set back from the road, inside of what looked like an old home.

I walked around to the side door and was rung in. The inside was not what I'd expected. It still had that homey vibe, but business had snuck in, probably sometime in the 1980s and then time stood still and nothing had been updated. The officer on my case was out so I sat to wait, reading every pamphlet on the wall, trying not to be nervous.

The Irish are funny. They have a winding way of speaking that I both appreciate and dislike. On the upside, it always feels like you're having a conversation, even with the doctor or the dentist, or, in this case, the police. It's not something you can rush. For instance, I just wanted to know why in God's name I was being called in! But you cannot rush to the point and must walk the winding roads leading to the knowledge you seek.

Turns out, drum roll please, I'd driven away without paying for gas outside of Cork City! When he finally returned, the officer pulled out a computer-printed photo of a still from a security camera. There I stood, not far from the door, in a petrol station, my hands on my hips.

I burst out laughing and sighed with relief.

I remembered what had happened.

I flew back to the States for Thanksgiving and to see family. While there I got super sick and extended my time so I wouldn't freak anyone out on the plane. I'd developed this strong cough (pre-Corona mind you), and I couldn't imagine sitting in close quarters with people. This meant that the turnaround time for my trip from Ireland to Kenya would be less than 48 hours.

I'd left my car parked at the Cork airport and when I touched down, exhausted and still semi-sick, I went to a petrol station outside of the city to fill up before the hour-and-a-half drive down West. I can still see myself there. Trying to pay at the pump, all American-like, and then remembering that I was in Ireland and had to go inside to pay.

I finished filling up and walked in. I stopped not far from the sliding doors and put my hands on my hips. I was deciding whether I wanted to buy a snack or not. Big thoughts I know! When I finally decided no, I spun around, walked out, and got in my car with absolutely no other thought in my mind than to get home. And I didn't give it another thought. Not one. Until I was shown the evidence.

Luckily, the gas station owner did not want to press charges. I called them immediately after leaving the station and spoke with a kind woman working the tills. She told me it happened *all* the time and there was nothing to worry about. I drove up that day to pay in full.

€67.32.

I was amazed – they didn't charge any fees for the inconvenience.

About a month later I got pulled over by the guards in Bantry. There was still a notice out on my car. And by notice, I mean whatever the Irish word is for criminal.

I explained my situation to the officer who pulled me over. I gave him names and dates. He let me go. That's one of the sweet things about living in a small town – if you're lying, they'll just come and find you. They know where you live.

I still have a photocopy of the still the police officer showed me that Solstice afternoon in Glengarriff. He made me promise not to share it with anyone. But I had it up on the corkboard by my front door for months afterward. A reminder of my closest brush with the Irish criminal justice system.

37

Little Moments

Have you ever seen tree glitter? It's a rare sighting.

I was unaware of its existence for a long time. It needs just the right angle of light, similar to rainbows, to become visible to the naked eye and catch a glimpse.

The first time I saw it I was driving towards my home in Ardna-trush. It was a warm afternoon and I felt that sleepy peacefulness you get in the car when all the windows are rolled up. As I approached the entrance to Seaview House there was a traffic jam, an uncommon occurrence in West Cork. I slowly stopped the car and waited in line and as I waited, I noticed why. Arborists, or tree surgeons as they're called in Ireland, were working alongside the road. I heard their saws buzzing and could almost anticipate their smell as they worked, a mix of sweat, diesel, and wood chips.

Then I noticed something else.

It looked like glitter floating through the air all around me. I blinked, my eyes attempting to focus – what was I seeing? Why was there glitter floating across the road here? Then it hit me. I began laughing. It was super fine sawdust from the cut trees – and as it floated down to the earth the sun caught its movement and turned it into tree glitter. I took a deep breath, the resinous scent of evergreens waking me up a little. Then traffic began moving again and I made my way along the coast towards home.

I love moments like this. They're small. They're poignant. Little stories like a patchwork quilt of beauty, humour, and unusualness.

Little moments.

I had another little moment in the Bantry library once. I liked to work in a corner towards the back. It had one wall made of glass with a view of the street above. That day a rainstorm came through and I watched as the glass in front of me gathered hundreds of raindrops, all hurtling downwards with riverine passion. That's when something else caught my eye – it's how it tends to be with these little moments. To my surprise, someone besides me was watching the storm. The library is tucked beside a hill, and I was lower down to the houses above. A man in tighty whities and a white wife beater tank top with a gold chain around his neck was also curious about the storm. His small frame filled the mini floor-to-ceiling window of his apartment. It made me laugh to catch him during this moment – I think it was the outfit.

Then there was the little boy who was peeing alongside the road. I was driving past the GAA club just outside of Bantry, and I saw him pacing, looking a little frantic. He looked around, lifted his shirt, tucked it right under his chin like I used to do as a child, turned slightly away from the road and began peeing right there in the parking lot, his tiny penis just over the waistline of his pants. It was a weird and funny thing to witness!

But sometimes, the moments are soulfully surprising.

One time I was exploring the sand dunes near Derrynane Beach in County Kerry. It's a beautiful place, off the beaten tourist track and filled with hiking trails to explore and a house shaped like a boat to wonder about. I climbed a sand dune and as I crested the ocean lay in front of me with the beach just below. I noticed a man creating geometric shapes in the sand using wooden tools. I walked down to meet him, got to hear his story, and learned something new that day about Sacred Geometry. But I'll never forget the amazement I felt when I saw him. It completely took me off guard.

Sometimes they are super mini little moments. A couple of breaths long.

Like the time I was parked at the top of Priest's Leap, a remote area of West Cork. I watched as tractor after tractor after tractor came out of the mist and crested the hill from the Kerry side, like a farming murder mystery, and disappeared back into the mist as they headed down towards the Cork side.

There was the time James Lyons almost watered me as he watered the window boxes at his shop.

Or the time I watched a black lab and a crow stare at each other at the Bantry Market. The crow was on the top of a six-foot wall and the dog was on the pavement below. What *were* they doing?

Ireland was rich in little moments for me. I think it's easier to attune to them in cultures that are more laid back. When things are more laid back, there's a tendency to feel relaxed, all of which helps you be in the present moment.

Let's explore three more.

#1: The Honey Bee

We sat on the side of the road by a beach, just talking, getting ready to go for a walk. We were talking about love. Oh, love. I was telling a story about someone I'd fallen in love with, in Ireland, to this man who I was falling in love with, in Ireland. He asked what happened and I said, "I guess it just wasn't meant to be."

At that precise moment, the moment after I finished my sentence, a honey bee flew into our van, right in front of us, and then out the other side.

We looked at each other.

"Did you see that??" I exclaimed.

"I said it wasn't meant to be and the bee!" I continued, confounded.

He laughed. He had a great laugh.

#2: Dursey Island Cable Car

Dursey Island is a beautiful place that sits off the coast of County Cork at the Southwestern end of the Beara Peninsula, about 700 feet from the mainland. That's about two-thirds the height of the Eiffel Tower. In 1969 a cable car was installed to cross the Dursey Sound. Though dolphin-rich, the currents make it treacherous to cross by boat. The 50 residents who called this place home at the time suddenly had a lifeline to the mainland. It wasn't uncommon to see sheep and cows being transported across back then!

Fast forward to the day I drove down to explore the island, now with a permanent population of 6. I rode in the cable car with a family of four. Two kids, a mum and a dad. The car can hold 6, just so you get an idea of the size. The kids had eyes on everything as we crossed, and I mean everything. The green of the island, the sun shining, the sheep in the fields, but then their noticings took a macabre turn.

"Look Dad, a dead seagull!" they exclaimed. Sure enough, a gull lay sprawled below us on the cable lines. Next, they became aware of the cracks in the floor beneath us. Our eyes were getting wider with each new discovery. But it was the holy water in the corner of the car that finally broke the ice, and we all began laughing. At least we had some protection!

#3: White Sage

I handed my friend a loose bunch of white sage for him to take home. He sat in his car wearing his red sweatshirt, he always wore that thing! He took the sage in his hands. He had the kinds of hands that had seen hard work – strong rough skin and a sense of dirt filling the ley lines, even when they were clean. He crushed the sage and took a deep breath. It was so beautiful. As I watched him,

I realised how connected he was to his senses. And how much he enjoyed the pungent scent as he took in the smell. It was like time slowed down and that ten-second moment felt triple in length.

Little moments like these make up the fabric of our lives, do you know what I mean? And beauty and mystery live in the space between our thoughts. They're like sunlight glimmering through the trees and reflecting off the water, like the electricity you feel just before a big storm, like the look in your lover's eyes as they gaze into you or that weirdo you saw riding a horse through downtown Seattle dressed up in costume.

When you start to notice little moments like this in your own life, be like my friend, okay? Take a few deep breaths and savour them. Let them touch you or make you laugh or wonder. And take a moment at the end of your day to remember them. They make life worth living. They really do.

38

The Catalyst of South Africa

Have you ever learned about something or experienced something new and then suddenly you start seeing it everywhere?

That's what happened to me with South Africa in West Cork.

One of my work clients introduced me to a friend in South Africa who was looking for help turning one of the books she'd written into an online course. After several weeks of connecting and negotiations, I decided to join her for a month in the bush as a consultant and partial volunteer! Needless to say, I was very excited. My trip to Kenya just months before had tamed my fear of travel in Africa and inspired me in a way I couldn't have imagined. So the idea of being back in the wilderness and exploring a new opportunity on this beautiful continent was so welcome.

The connections to South Africa started happening slowly and in small ways – newspaper articles and mentions of the country by people I knew. But it was when I spoke with my landlady's gardener that the connections started to intensify. Turns out he had a strong South African connection. He told me he'd met his wife there. They were both Irish, from different counties, and ran into each other as volunteers in Lesotho, a mountain kingdom inside the borders of South Africa. He'd been to Kruger National Park and encouraged me to be very careful. People were getting attacked by lions there he said! I really hope he didn't see the scepticism on my face that day.

To his credit, he wasn't completely wrong. I did some research and discovered there had been a couple of human/lion encounters in which the human hadn't fared so well. A blog post detailed one such encounter where a guide misjudged the body language of a lioness, and her bluff charge turned into a real one. Photos of her mangled arm followed. The photos were shocking and a reality check. The attacks, however, were rare and that made me feel better.

I arrived in South Africa, known as the Rainbow Nation, on February 14th, 2019. With the lion attacks distant in my mind and a more real fear emerging, that of snakes, I started to settle in at the conservation project ready to dive in and create.

The experience was not what I'd imagined based on all of the pre-conversations and negotiations. In fact, it was disappointing. Until it wasn't. I ended up meeting people who changed my life! It was here I learned about the Field Guides Association of Southern Africa and its comprehensive safari guide training system. The moment I heard about it I knew, in this quiet space inside, that I was going to do one of their qualification programs. I've only had this feeling a few times in my life, so when it arrives, I welcome it.

I spent the month with the sounds of hyenas calling, lions roaring, crickets strimming, and the biggest fireflies I've ever seen in my life filling the night air. Sunrise and sunset brought on a richness of bird life I'd never experienced before and, despite the intense heat that felt like it was cooking me from the inside out, I started to fall in love with South Africa.

Four weeks later I flew back to Ireland. And woke up with an ache in my heart.

The wildness of the bush had sunk into a deep part of me and even the beauty of the peninsulas and ocean waters of West Cork paled in comparison. I'd make coffee that I purchased in South Africa every morning, drink it from a beautiful mug covered in wild animals that I got in Kruger National Park, and text with a new guy I'd started dating who was from Cape Town. And that's when the South Africa connections in West Cork really started to ramp up!

Suddenly and seemingly out of nowhere, I was meeting South Africans! It's like they heard this new love song inside of me and started appearing out of nowhere, right on my path.

The lady at The Black Cat in Glengarriff who was from SA and had married an Irish man. The woman in Bantry who was from Somerset West and had emigrated to Ireland and started a flower shop. My friend messaged and told me he was cutting trees on a property owned by South Africans! I met a couple from Zimbabwe or Rhodesia as they still called it and another man who was from Zim as well. It wasn't just South Africa showing up – Africa was representing!

About a week after I returned my landlady told me a woman was going to be moving in, to the flat next door to me. Her name was Ingrid and she'd recently lost her husband and needed a new place to live. When we finally met I discovered, not only was she a portrait artist, but from Cape Town, born and bred! I was in awe.

She and I became friends. One night I went over to hers for dinner. She made bobotie, a unique South African Cape Malay curry with mince and raisins, topped with egg. We sat drinking G&Ts as the sun set and finished the night with a very American blueberry pie for dessert. Ingrid was a magical woman and had beautiful paintings all over her home. And I felt like South Africa stayed with me as I navigated my life in Ireland.

In August of 2019, less than half a year after my first trip to South Africa, I finally followed that quiet voice inside and signed up for my Level 1 Field Guide Course with a long-standing company called EcoTraining. And in late January of 2020 flew back to South Africa. This time to Cape Town. While that guy and I weren't seeing each other anymore, he had sent me so many beautiful pictures of Cape Town, his home place, that I knew I needed to spend some time there before my course.

In October of 2019 I sublet my flat in Ireland and went back to the US to spend some time with my mom. She'd just lost her long-term partner and I wanted to be there for her. My intention was to stay in Ohio until I left for my course and then come back to Ireland after I graduated.

It's funny looking back. Life really did have other plans. Covid-19 was about to hit the world by storm. I can remember sitting in my mom's living room the night before my flight to South Africa. It was snowing. A lot. And my friend Amber came over to say goodbye. As we chatted in the living room, the TV on mute, I saw headlines of a virus coming out of China, with worries about its effects on the world. In retrospect Amber already had a pulse on the situation and as a goodbye gift brought me gummy bears for the plane. And masks. A whole pack of them. The snow, the news, and Amber's masks made me start to worry. I popped a gummy bear into my mouth. What was I getting myself into? But I knew in my heart that I was going to make the trip, go over and take it from there.

I arrived in Cape Town at night. It wasn't until the morning that the complete and utter beauty and magic of this city filled my eyes. I took the Hop On, Hop Off bus tour to get a big-picture view of everything. There were mountains, everywhere! Bright, sparkling oceans. And people of all kinds of colours filled the streets – markedly different from Ireland and West Cork. I felt like I was coming out of a dream. A backwater. And entering the flow of life again. It felt so good.

About a month into my course in the bush the South African government announced that it was going into full lockdown. We were up in the very northeast of the country in the middle of nowhere in Kruger National Park learning about aardvark tracks and elephant behaviour and walking on foot in Big 5 areas. Across one of the rivers, we could even see Zimbabwe! So this announcement hit all of us hard. Suddenly we had 48 hours to book flights home and exit the country or enter lockdown with all South Africans.

It was one of my wildest travel experiences to date and everything started moving very quickly. At first, we thought we might be able to stay and finish our course and just go into lockdown there. Then we found out that South African Parks said if we did stay, we'd have to isolate in our cabins and couldn't gather together to learn. Then just as quickly it changed again, the park closed all entry gates, and we'd need to leave with proof of a flight out of the country. We were scrambling!

One afternoon we drove to Pafuri Gate to get better reception so all of us could book our flights. And the gates were shut. Closed. Locked. I'm unsure if that has ever actually happened in South Africa before. It was totally eerie.

Next, we packed in haste, drove 10 and a half hours down to Joburg, and spent the night near the airport. I'd booked my flight out of Cape Town because all my South African friends told me that if you get stuck in South Africa, Cape Town was the place to be. I'd been planning to drive down with one of my instructors. But you know what? The plans kept changing! He came to me; told me he'd booked a flight down to Cape Town because he didn't think we'd make it in time for the lockdown deadline. "You better book yourself a flight too," he said. "Hopefully there's one left!"

I was shocked. And angry. But hopped on my computer and booked one of the last remaining flights down to Cape Town the next morning. Looking back, it was actually perfect. My own flight time out of the country changed from the day after lockdown to the night before and if we'd driven, I would never have made it in time. It taught me how important letting go of plans and being in the moment is during emergency situations. It's best to just go with what's happening and make the next best possible decision.

I can still remember sitting outside the airport waiting for my flight. Table Mountain was in view, the sun setting, everything so beautiful. I did not want to leave. The hustle and bustle of the people were all around me, they were wrapping up their day early to go home to family and friends and the great unknown. There was something so innocent about it all. Like the majority of us had no idea what was about to happen to our world.

I chose to fly back to the US instead of Ireland. I wanted to be with my mom during this crazy time. The woman who was subletting my apartment decided to stay and shelter in place. So I spent the next 5 months in Ohio.

During this time of suspended animation, as the world slowed and then came to the biggest stop I've ever experienced in my life, I got clear about me and Ireland. It was time for me to leave. I just knew it in my heart and soul.

In late August 2020 I found a gap in the lockdowns and flew back to Ireland to pack up my stuff and move back to the

States. I'd already decided to return to South Africa in 2021 to redo my course, this time with another company called Nature Guide Training. They had connections to my former employer Wilderness Awareness School and focused on tracking as a big part of their curriculum. I had a feeling they'd be a better fit for me than EcoTraining.

When I arrived in Ireland the quarantine requirement was two weeks. Strangely, this was kind of perfect. There was no pressure to socialise. I outlined the entirety of Rainbow Weather, the book you're now reading, from my stone cottage by the sea overlooking the Beara Peninsula. It flowed out of me like water. In between I worked and packed up all my stuff.

When quarantine was over I spent the next four weeks continuing my work, saying goodbye to my friends and favourite places, and beginning to make peace with my time in Ireland. This process would end up taking about two years and the unfolding of this book to actually find consistent true peace inside with all my adventures there.

I did make it back to South Africa in 2021. I'm still in awe that all the changing regulations allowed for it. I kept my going with the flow lesson during emergency situations lesson right in the forefront of my brain and surfed the ever-shifting Covid landscape. I began to develop a keen intuition and trust that it was going to work out. And it did! In late January 2021 I flew, once again, to Cape Town. A couple of days later I made my way to the bush, and eventually finished my course, qualifying as a Level 1 Field Guide in the FGASA system and a Level 1 Tracker in the CyberTracker system. It was one of the proudest moments of my life.

I now call South Africa home. And I wrote this story with the view of Table Mountain out the window of my apartment. She is so beautiful. If you get a chance, go and visit the mountain. You'll see what I mean when you arrive.

Work

"Slow, ticking, beautiful time."

-Kat Koch

I flew to Ireland with the promise of a working holiday visa for one year and left the Garda station with a stamp on my passport for two! During my entire time working in this country, I never once filled out a job application. I handed in a CV. Twice. Mostly, the process of getting hired was kind of like this: Go in, have a chat with the owner, if they liked your energy, you'd get a trial day, and then boom! You had a job.

I had the pleasure of doing many different kinds of jobs. From life drawing modelling to landscaping and even a stint as a cashier at a local petrol station come supermarket. Eventually I transitioned into becoming a virtual assistant, a job that gave me location independence *and* travel opportunities.

Something I'd been dreaming of for years.

39

Always Believe Something Wonderful is about to Happen

O ver the years I've come to realise that what was about to happen between Bernie and me was totally normal in my world. A daily occurrence in the best possible way.

But according to the raised eyebrows I received from others across race, culture, and gender? Not always the case. Nope. I've learned this isn't the norm.

Call it what you will:

Alignment

Magic

Synchronicity

Kismet

Fate

Destiny

Luck

Chance

I love all these words!

Bernie and I were about to make some magic, and this was only the start of it.

I walked into the Stuffed Olive and immediately the smell of coffee met me – bitter, sweet, and creamy scents filling my nose. I began to drool. It was busy, but I didn't mind. It was one of two places that made me forget I'd ever lived in the Seattle area – their coffee was that good! I ordered a flat white as my eyes drifted over Portuguese Custards and Lemon Madeira Cakes and freshly baked Fruit Scones.

The coffee machine whirred, and I noticed a young woman with silky brown hair tied up in a wavy ponytail in front of it. It was like she was dancing even though she barely moved, frothing the milk and then swirling it to make that perfect flat white consistency. She had a glint in her eye, and that glint caught mine. As I waited for my order, I began to make conversation because, well, glint! Her name was Bernie O Sullivan.

I wish I could remember our conversation word for word. But I can't. What I do remember was that after some fun pleasantries, I mentioned I was looking for work and Bernie mentioned that Manning's Emporium was hiring staff for the season.

Manning's! I loved the coffee at Manning's – it was my other favourite place to get warm and caffeinated. She gave me one of the owner's numbers and within a few days I'd scheduled an interview. Wow, who knew coffee could be so fruitful?

Manning's Emporium is a West Cork institution. They support and promote small, local artisan food producers and have some of the best charcuterie and cheese plates I've ever tasted. They're a family-run business and have been since their inception, each generation building on the work of the past to stay relevant and passionate. I was excited for my interview!

It was a sunny day when I walked into their café and shop, the normal hustle and bustle had died down to quiet. Andrew, one of the owners, met me just inside by a little bar table that isn't there anymore. I handed him my CV and his deep brown eyes scanned the page.

"Bernie O Sullivan told me you were hiring! I've always loved this place, especially the coffee – I'd love to hear more about the job."

Andrew smiled.

"Ah Bernie, she's great. Yeah, so we're looking for a barista and waitress for the tourist season. 32 hours a week and we pay minimum wage. What kind of experience do you have?" he asked.

I was upfront, "Well, I was a barista as a teenager, so it's been a while! I've been involved in customer service most of my life, love people, love to learn and I'm usually pretty quick at picking up new skills."

We chatted for no more than three minutes. I guess he liked my vibe! Because Andrew told me to come in over the weekend for a trial day and if it felt like a good fit between us, I'd have the job.

It was the easiest interview I'd ever had. This would be a repeating theme in Ireland. It seemed that the connection was just as important, if not more, than the qualifications when it came down to it. Job interviews can feel so stiff and official. This felt natural. Simple. Easy. Open. And full of potential.

A week later I went to see Bernie at the Stuffed Olive again. I thanked her for telling me about the opportunity and that I got the job! Then, a thought hit me.

"Bernie, so I'm doing this thing where I go upside down, like in a handstand, once a day in a cool spot. Would you take my picture for today? That waterwheel at the library looks perfect."

Bernie smiled her bright smile, the one I'd be lucky enough to get a chance to know and love. Then she took her apron off and nearly sashayed down the street with me to take the photo. And because it's just who she is, she ended up going upside down with me!

A few days later she sent me a meme with a black background and lots of exposed lightbulbs hanging from a theatre ceiling. Here's what it said:

Always believe that something wonderful is about to happen.

I smiled. A slow, spreading smile. I could feel my body turn warm and gooey at the thought. It was illogical in the best possible way.

And that my readers is how I got my first job in Ireland. And how this new friendship, one between an American optimist and an Irish one, began.

40

Kat, is that you on the Wall?

We were at a pop-up restaurant in Ballydehob, enjoying a fancy meal in a very simple and stark setting.

I was so happy to be with my friends eating this beautiful food, that the environment hadn't fully sunken into my conscious mind.

Then I saw Cian shift his gaze my way, his body partly turned towards the wall away from us. Softly and subtly, as only he could do, he said "Kat, is that you?" and pointed. I looked up.

On the grey wall were four very large drawings, all of the same naked woman. He was only pointing to one, however after a quick scan, I could tell that the four pencil sketches were indeed me. Full of my curves and signature flip bun.

You see, during my time in Ireland I'd become a life drawing model to earn extra cash and kind of fell in love with the whole thing. Initially what drew me towards it was the living hourly wage paid to models, €25 or about $28 per hour at the time. I'd tried it once before in a local art studio when I lived in the Pacific NW. It was like doing yoga for two hours, connecting and breathing, and trying to keep the poses alive and glowing. And I found that the artists loved my curves.

The same became true for me in Ireland.

My first modelling gig was down at the Skibbereen Arts Centre about 40 minutes south from where I was living. I was so nervous. They'd asked me to bring a robe or gown to wear in-between drawing sessions. I'd showered and shaved and dreamed up some poses to share. But walking into that art room full of the smells that only an art room can possess, like clay and paper, charcoal and eraser, I felt butterflies in my stomach.

Slowly a group of older artists began filling the room, setting up their easels, and collecting their big paper and thick charcoal pencils. I knew no one there. Thank God! This was West Cork after all. My best friend's mom could have shown up and it wouldn't have surprised me.

And so, eventually, I got naked. I posed for short bursts. And longer bursts. And even laid down for a full 45 minutes, listening as their pencils shuffled and scratched on the dense paper. My arm started to fall asleep, stretched out under my head, but I just kept breathing. I didn't want to interrupt the flow, so I challenged myself to stay with it.

I've noticed there is a rhythm to life drawing classes. Teachers like to give their students different time lengths to practise their skills. The shorter times help artists to get out of their heads and simply draw what they see. And the longer ones give them time to practise the skills they are learning as they make shapes.

Often when the teachers spoke, I'd find myself inspired by what they said. I understood how their words related to art, but I also found they related to life. Things like:

"She's using the mistakes she makes as strengths."

"She gets lost in an area sometimes and forgets the whole."

"Be as honest as possible and be prepared to change."

Needless to say, I loved modelling. And I was good at it. Students would tell me so, both inside and outside of class. And that's where this story will eventually lead us back to that pop-up restaurant in Ballydehob. So, stay with me!

After my first class down in Skibbereen I travelled another 50 minutes north to a nature reserve in Glengarriff to explore and get some air. I'd had a great day and walking through the oak woodlands was just adding to the pleasure.

Suddenly, a small, brown dog trotted up to me. I reached down to give some love when a woman and a man came over the rise in front of me. I stood up and smiled. Then I heard her say with a big grin, "Great class today!" When she saw my look of bewilderment she said, "Oh! Maybe I shouldn't have said that?" And then I knew where I'd seen her. She was one of the artists from the morning's class!

You can imagine my amazement. What are the odds? We laughed and I told her thank you and off we went on our separate ways. Chalk it up to coincidence, but this wasn't the only time this kind of thing happened.

I was once walking around Kenmare with a friend. We were getting ready to cross the street when suddenly, I felt this person come up behind me, put her arm on my shoulder, kiss me on the cheek and say, "Such a great session today!" Then without any kind of conversation, she continued on her way, crossing the street in front of us.

I looked over at my friend – bewilderment again! I had absolutely no idea who she was; she took me by complete surprise. Ten minutes later I finally figured it out.

Which leads us back to myself, Cian, and my other friend Jean eating in a restaurant, sketches of me on the wall. After I laughed, I got a little heated. Consent, anyone? Never once did it occur to me that any of the sketches done in class would later be used for a show or commercial purposes.

So, I decided to do what any self-respecting naked art model would do and phoned up the pop-up restaurant owner. I explained the situation. After *his* laughter died down, only to be replaced with a similar small shock, I asked him for the artist's name. He phoned back a couple of days later. It was a woman who shall remain nameless and who I didn't know.

I never contacted her. But I did learn that I should always ask if an artist plans on having their sketches shown in public. To be honest, I didn't *really* mind. I just would have preferred a heads-up. As you've seen in this story, West Cork is a small place, and you never know who you're going to run into – including yourself!

41

A Little Museum Full of Wonders

He cancelled on me. Again.

I sat in my car, slightly depressed, looking out towards the ocean.

What was I going to do now?

I laid back in the seat and contemplated my fate. It didn't look good, just disappointment with wheels.

Strange though, Ireland is a magic place. You've heard me say it before now, but it seems to respond very well to energy – what you want, what you don't want, what you need, and maybe even what challenges you. It's all there, swirling around for you at any moment, waiting for a thread or hook of your intention to reach out and grasp it. I genuinely don't know how it works.

I do know that the more rigid you become the fewer opportunities seem to present themselves.

But in this moment by the sea, sitting with my disappointment, my phone made the double bell sound alerting me to a message on Viber. Someone was trying to get my attention.

Inside I found an invite for a night of music at Levis Corner House in Ballydehob from my friend Bernie. I thought, fuck it, why not? And found myself responding with a yes. And just like that, plans went from one thing to another, and off I drove down the N-71 to the village.

I love Levis's. As one of the current owners calls it, it is indeed "a little museum full of wonders". The shelves and walls are filled with antiques – from paintings to figurines to old-school groceries. You could bring a child (or my cousin for that matter) in here and keep them occupied for weeks, discovering all the hidden treasures inside.

It's also the kind of place Jeremy Irons frequents. Many celebrities love West Cork because the Irish, especially those in remote villages, honestly don't care about your fame. Mostly they just ignore you or treat you like any other person walking down the street or having a pint.

One time I was at Levis's for a gig when I saw an odd-looking man, almost homeless in appearance, with a small white dog in his lap. I watched in fascination as he took one of the clear glass candle holders, removed all the stones from inside it, and poured water from his water bottle into it. He then proceeded to let his dog lap and lap and lap the light water into its pink mouth. It was like a train wreck; I couldn't look away.

When the gig ended my friend Kenny started talking to the man as he exited.

"Who is that guy?" I asked Kenny after he'd gone.

"Kat!!! That is Jeremy Irons!" he said.

Oh. Right. Guess I'm more Irish than I let on.

Owned by the same family for the last 100 years, Levis's has been taken over in recent times by a young couple who are trying to bring life back to the pub, the business, and the village itself with brand-new events, shows, and even food trucks in the summertime.

And that's what had brought me out the night I was supposed to hang out with Cian and instead found myself in the Levis pub with Bernie. Listening to bluegrass music.

As the gig wound down and I waited for my brown-haired friend to give her long, Irish goodbyes, I went into one of the back rooms and sat down. Near me was a good-looking guy with J. Crew, floppy model hair, and a red sweatshirt. He looked nice so I started talking to him. Turns out he was from California and off we went on our American speak about living life abroad. And whether Trump would actually win the upcoming presidential election. We were convinced he wouldn't.

Then I casually mentioned I was looking for work.

"What do you want to do? " Seth asked me (Seth was his name by the way).

I listed off a slew of skills which included gardening and within 5 minutes I had a promise from him to contact his boss. He worked for a landscaping company, and they were looking for more people to add to their crew. Two days later I had my first trial day. And then a full-time job which consisted of regular laughter with 6 other guys, pulling weeds, digging, and sometimes even planting trees in the rainy Irish winter. I loved it.

Thank you, Cian, for cancelling our plans that day. And thank you Bernie for inviting me along on your musical adventure. Without you both my disappointment on wheels could have been way longer lasting.

42

The Dúchas of Yoga

It seemed like everywhere I turned there were yoga teachers in West Cork. I'd meet a new person and bam! They taught yoga.

I'd pass a community board, bam! Yoga classes were being taught, from Allihies all the way to Goleen.

"Where did all of these yoga teachers come from?" I wondered, being one myself!

By the time I moved to Ireland, I'd been teaching for 5 years. I was living in Washington State when I got inspired by a local yogini and studio owner in my community. She was the rare kind of teacher who made yoga feel truly accessible, not only to me, but to everybody in her classes. She made jokes. She was supportive. And she inspired me with her practice. She listened to her body, was creative in exploring modifications, and totally capable of doing really fun poses like Scissors, Dragonfly or Head to Ankle. Yoga began to feel real, no longer holier than thou or Guru-esque. Just a practice to learn, heal, grow, and expand.

When I moved to the Bantry area I didn't expect to find yoga teachers scattered like a dazzle of zebras on the grasslands, absolutely everywhere! But they were. And it turns out, yoga found its way to the shores of West Cork back in the late 1970s, becoming more prominent in the early 80s.

In fact, West Cork has been a convergence of cultures for hundreds of years. From Algerian pirates attacking the village of Baltimore to new-age hippies emigrating from a tense Maggie Thatcher's England, quirk and variety have been present on this landscape for a very long time.

So, I did what any quirky American yoga teacher would do – I joined them!

I started off teaching a weekly class at the Alice West Centre, way down on the Sheep's Head Peninsula. Almost everyone who attended was over 60 and all of them had different levels of flexibility and mobility. I decided to teach my first-ever chair yoga series to help mitigate the truly all levels nature of the students. We'd sit in a circle doing Eagle arms, Uddiyana Bandha, and wide-legged twists in fold-out chairs normally reserved for church potlucks. It was one of my favourite days of the week and I loved the challenge of working with women whose needs were so different from the students I'd worked with before.

As I taught, and learned more about the yogic landscape of West Cork, I began to realise it was quite different to my experiences in the American one. Teachers tended towards offering a series of classes lasting 6 to 8 weeks, with a commitment required upfront for the whole thing. Teachers also held classes in varied locations, from hotels to gyms to community halls. There was no yoga-only studio when I first arrived there. Although there had been.

It was and still is called An Sanctóir or the Sanctuary in Irish. Born from some of the earliest adopters and teachers of yoga in the region, it opened its doors in 1996. Over the years it turned into a holistic community centre offering all kinds of classes, workshops, and music events. It also hosted a yearly yoga festival that began in 2016!

I spoke with Charlie Stevens, one of the founders of An Sanctóir and a grandfather to yoga in West Cork, to find out more about the early days. Charlie was born in England and began studying yoga with the British Wheel before accidentally moving to Ireland in 1975. He and his crew sailed over on an around-the-world test voyage, and he loved it so much he ended up staying. Forever. He never took that trip.

Upon arrival, he found very little yoga. A woman called Marianne Gabriel was teaching classes in Clonakilty, that was it. He said something that really struck me. Even though there weren't many classes on the landscape like modern-day West Cork, he felt like yoga was already present there. He kinned yoga to harmony. Or being in alignment with oneself. He met many people in his new home who seemed genuinely content and at ease in themselves and felt in harmony with life, nature, and their relationships. Maybe that's why yoga found such an easy home in this part of Ireland?

From quirk to harmony, I began taking classes from different teachers. I loved the variety of people and styles to be found in the area – you could practise yoga most days of the week!

Then something cool happened.

Erin Kelly Ashworth opened a yoga studio in Bantry and asked me to teach there. Erin spent a lot of time in Cleveland, Ohio growing up and experienced the American style of running a studio, so her new venture was modelled after that. Students could take all kinds of styles of classes from different teachers under one roof! They could buy class passes and drop in whenever they'd like.

Most people loved this new concept. But a few were wary. I'll never forget when a local farmer, who had been coming to my classes weekly, both when I taught in Durrus and when I moved to the studio, asked me if he could go to someone else's class.

"What do you mean?" I asked, curious.

He was soft-spoken, this farmer.

"Well, um, ya know, would it be okay, ya know, if I take other people's classes, not just yours?"

It was then I realised there was a sense of not only loyalty but obligation between yoga teacher and student here. It reminded me of a situation one of my friends found himself in. He got upset that someone who was in his same trade took a job with one of his clients and didn't ask permission first. My friend didn't have time for the work but had the expectation that since their colleague knew this person was his client, they should ask.

I was *not* used to this. Not in the slightest. In the US, if you don't have time, you understand that job is up for grabs. As I juggled these cultural differences in my mind I was torn between respect and ridiculousness. I also began to realise why it took so long to get things done in West Cork!

"Of course, you can," I said to the farmer. "That's what this studio is all about!"

He never came back to my classes after that.

I knew it wasn't personal. I knew he liked them. And I don't know why he never returned. But I'm so glad he felt free to do his thing, unencumbered by any expectation he may have thought I had.

I have to say, it was kinda sweet that he asked.

Yoga has always been a practice of connection for me. And that's why I loved teaching it. It helped me feel like I could come home to myself, and through that intrinsic belonging, it brought me into a deeper connection with the natural world and the people I was in community with.

Ireland is a place of belonging. Some people never leave their village. Or county. They know every rock, tree, and hedge. They are woven together with family, neighbours, and nature, a kind of existence I know little about, being a global citizen.

This is something Charlie and I naturally gravitated towards during our conversation when I interviewed him. He told me a funny story right at the end that highlights this sense of belonging. He was having a drink with a friend in the pub, sharing stories back and forth, as you do. His friend's neighbour had been pulled over by the cops. When they came up to his window, he asked why he'd been pulled over. The Gardai told him he'd forgotten to put his indicator light on when he was turning right.

The man paused.

"Ah sure," he said, "everyone knows I'm turning there anyway."

I swear, I was still laughing when I ended that Zoom call with Charlie.

My friend Bernie told me that when she was a little one, her mom used a turn of phrase that she's only now understanding.

"Oh, that's the dúchas coming out of him (or her)."

Dúchas is an Irish word. It means homeland, place, ancestral home. Essentially, it's a word of belonging.

The more I learned about Ireland and yoga, the more I began to believe that maybe Charlie was right. The essence of yoga was indeed present on the Irish landscape long before the practice found its way there from India. Maybe India and Ireland are soul sisters.

43

Backroads

The backroads of West Cork and South Kerry are fantastic.

While Ireland, for all intents and purposes, is a modern country, its roads still harken back to the days of the horse and wagon. What would pass for a one-lane road in America is definitely a 2-way thoroughfare, to be sped down as quickly as possible. Beautiful hedges full of wildflowers such as fuchsia, meadowsweet, and this cool little puff of a blue flower that I have yet to identify, line the road, sometimes on both sides. They require a newfound faith in yourself and humanity. They also require a keen eye and good memory for the sparsely populated pullovers, for those times you meet another car head-on.

I love to drive. I listen to music. Explore. Destress. Sometimes I'd do all three while driving the little hidden lanes within an hour of my home. Because I'd discovered so many cool things (like ruins and giant boulders and lakes) every time I passed a road I'd never been down, I'd save it for one of those days when all I wanted to do was drive.

And backroads were just backroads. Until one day, the word evolved into a new meaning for me.

I was working at Manning's Emporium when a small group of very fit humans came in to have food and drinks. They sat up the back and I was immediately drawn to them. They were having a great time, lots of laughter and joking. Taking their order got me laughing and made my day. They were a mix of American, English, and Irish people and they worked for a company called, now wait for it, Backroads.

Backroads is an active adventure travel company based in the United States that facilitates trips all over the world. I mean *all* over, even Tibet! They have one of the highest customer return rates for their industry and employ some seriously amazing people, as I was now witnessing.

I ended up exchanging phone numbers with one of the women and suddenly a new income stream and new friends were born!

Eventually, these same people who worked for Backroads hired me as a contractor to teach yoga to their bicycle trip leaders as a form of self-care and recovery after their trips. The work they do is full-on, physically, emotionally, and mentally, so stretching, relaxation and someone else guiding them were very welcome and needed. I used to drive to Kenmare and meet them at the Park Hotel Spa a few times a month. One time I even taught some of their participants!

I loved working with them. I'd create a themed yoga class based on their recovery needs and teach them in the dimly lit, underground yoga room of the hotel. It was peaceful. And so rewarding.

These people were hungry for help, fit and body aware enough to really understand what I shared as a teacher. There's a kind of spark and energetic flow that builds in classes like these and I usually ended up with more energy afterwards than I had before.

These same people also taught me about their weird and wonderful world of cycling. I discovered incredibly lightweight bikes, how my legs felt like hot honey after 14 km of cycling with them on the backroads outside Kenmare, and what great senses of humour they had; I'd laugh for hours at some of their house parties.

My friend encouraged me to apply for a trip leader position within the company. I was hesitant. I wasn't a cyclist! I didn't know the first thing about leading a cycling trip. But she said that leadership style and people skills were more important.

So I applied and after making it through a series of interviews, flew to Paris for one in-person. We had both one-on-one and group sessions as part of the application process.. We had to perform on-the-spot bike repairs, on-the-spot analyses of potential situations with guests, and speak in front of everyone about who we were and what we could bring to Backroads.

It was the hardest interview I've ever been through. And unfortunately, I just couldn't cut it. I was not accepted as a trip leader.

That interview was, however, a personal milestone for me. It was one of the most honest interviews I've ever given, one in which I didn't pretend to be anything other than myself. I felt proud of that. My own disappointment was softened by that. And by the fact that not only was the experience a new and interesting one, I'd met amazing people and learned a lot about myself. And bikes! Changing a punctured air tube when you're being timed is surprisingly hard!

I did continue to teach yoga to the trip leaders, spend time with them outside work, and enjoy running into them in the small towns surrounded by some of Ireland's most beautiful backroads.

44

Retreat to Ireland

E verything sparkles. Eyes. Spider webs heavy with dew. Grains of sand. Reflections in lakes. Even a crust of bread left to dry in the warm autumn light.

Everything sparkles. Like the unbridled laugh of a child, like the blooming of a flower, like the words of a sincere prayer. Like memories held dear in the heart and mind.

Memories from my Retreat to Ireland are like that. They sparkle, filling me up like warm, bubbling water. And remind me of one of my undeniable personal truths – that life is an adventure, an experiment, and a journey all rolled into one.

I created this retreat for many reasons. I loved to travel. I loved Ireland. I was a yoga teacher. But one of the main reasons was because I wanted to create experiences where people could step away from their day-to-day realities and have such amazing adventures they'd go home lit up from within. My hope was that that light would inspire them to show up in their life differently. Or change it altogether!

As a teenager, I was regularly bored by adults. It seemed most of them weren't present. Stuck in routines and ruts. And, at the very least, semi-unhappy and disconnected from life. I used to hide in the branches of the maple tree outside of my childhood home, tucked up amongst the amber brown leaves. I'd sit there, barely visible, to see if anybody walking by would notice me. 9 times out of 10 they didn't. This further reinforced my disdain for adulthood.

Now, having become one myself, not a normal one by any standards, but one nonetheless, I realise why so many adults are unhappy. Life isn't easy! Stuff happens. Plus, you must provide for yourself, and maybe a family and all of it adds up. It can become easy to forget about the deeper, more meaningful aspects of life when you're caught up paying the bills or trying to survive.

And so, eventually, my Retreat to Ireland was born.

It was bespoke before bespoke was a thing. I called it an adventure of unrepeatable magic. Ireland herself inspired that sentence. She'd shown me again and again that you couldn't predict what was right around the corner. Many times, it was something surprising and completely delightful. If you could let go just enough of some of your structure and planning, you'd get so much more fulfilment.

This was a challenge for an international retreat, so I kept it small. Eight people max. Much easier to move a smaller group on the fly than a big one. Each retreat had the themes of yoga, nature, and culture, and from there I'd custom-create itineraries for the people who signed up. I'd connect with each participant about their passions and why they wanted to come to Ireland, and then

I'd use that as inspiration to create the schedule for the week. Sometimes I'd read in between the lines of what they shared and offer up something surprising. And sometimes I'd notice an overall theme developing for the week and create from that space.

I know some of my customers wished for a little more structure. And I get why. They were flying across the pond to a new country, with people they didn't know, to go on an adventure. I can understand why they'd want to cross all their t's and dot all their i's. Still, I knew in my soul, a little chaos brings experiences that aren't soon forgotten.

Take Katie. Katie was on my first retreat, a group of 3 women, all from the Snoqualmie Valley where I lived at the time. We spent a week walking along the Sheep's Head Peninsula, set dancing, having an impromptu yoga session on a windy beach and saving a lamb caught in a fence!

When it was time for Katie to head back to Dublin to catch her flight, she had a plan. My friend Sheila would drop her off in Bandon on her way to work, she could catch the bus to Cork, get on the train to Dublin and make her way to the airport from there. Thing is, chaos had a different plan. And to this day, Katie says it is one of her favourite memories from the trip.

She caught that lift with Sheila and was dropped off in Bandon near the bus stop. While she waited, she crossed the street to grab a snack and something to drink for the ride. The lady at the register noticed Katie and her large 40-pound travel backpack and asked where she was headed.

Katie told me she will never forget the look on that woman's face when she said she was catching the bus to Cork and then on to Dublin via train.

"Oh deary," she said, "the buses are on strike. You won't be catching any bus today."

When the kind woman noticed Katie's frightened face, she sprang into action and helped organise a lift to the city with a nearby patron. And though Katie didn't know her, or the man she was about to get in the car with, she did what most of us tend to do in Ireland; she trusted.

She stepped hesitantly into the small two-door, faded red, hatchback with a short, stocky gentleman who had the thickest Irish accent she'd ever heard. The drive took an hour, Katie couldn't understand a word he said and then he dropped her off about a mile from the train station. She had to hoof it to make her train, but she made it!

I asked Katie about this moment. Here's what she said: "I remember smiling and shaking my head thinking about the morning and what had just occurred. This is what it's all about! Travelling brings people and problem-solving and happy accidents into your life that you don't expect. *Those are the memories that you'll never forget.*"

See what I mean? A little bit of chaos does a soul good.

Over the course of six years, I ran five separate retreats. Every year a new series of adventures revealed themselves. We had Burt and

Annie Moran over for a set dancing lesson, went night swimming off Snave Pier, and sea kayaking around Glengarriff Harbor with a local guide who had us drink homemade wine from inside the kayaks. We went dolphin watching and even took a private boat trip around the Lakes of Killarney, stopping at an old-growth woodland only accessible by water. We went night kayaking in bioluminescence, learned the basics of stone carving using only hand tools with Victor Daly and walked the hedgerows gathering plants for salve making and a wildcrafted cocktail night.

We ate Thai food cooked by an Irish woman, spent time in the pubs listening to music and even went to a "locals only" storytelling night in which we were welcomed like we belonged. See what I mean by sparkling?

I felt so proud of Retreat to Ireland. And I loved supporting local businesses. I partnered with local people, both in West Cork and the Rebel County at large to bring the magic of Ireland to my clients. I invited them to come and not only awaken their senses but get lost with me in Ireland.

I knew I'd hit that sweet spot, enough structure to create containment, but simultaneously enough space to allow the magic to unfold when Molly wrote to me years later. Here's what she said:

"I'm going through the photos again right now because I finally have a home where I can print and hang some and it's bringing such beautiful heart smiles back to me. What a trip that was. Magical, sweet, soothing. It felt like every single adventure was hand-picked just for us.... because they were! I didn't feel like I was in some tourist box checking type of trip. I've been on those and came out of them surprisingly angry - feeling misled. Not this trip. This was authenticity at the core. Home. It ignited a flame long lost."

Yes! I wanted to create transformational and healing experiences for people without calling them such. It's always been my way. Healing through adventure, fun and direct experiences with life. Even back in my early years of teaching yoga I'd grown bored and disenchanted with the way the wellness industry did and still does along with so many other capitalist ventures – make people think there's something wrong with them so they'll buy something. No! I wanted something that helped people reconnect, to themselves, to other people and to the natural world.

My friend Rosalee said it best after her experience both as a participant and teacher in 2017: "I went on the Retreat to Ireland with Kat in the hopes of having a restful vacation in a country I've often felt drawn towards. What I was not expecting was the transformational experience I went through. Ireland lured me in with its beautiful hedgerows and fun and witty people. And through Kat's guidance, this retreat was more than a scrapbook trip. Connecting to a place through the culture and the natural world gave me an opportunity for inward reflection that has continued to have a big influence on my life months later."

So, let me ask you this...

You're standing in front of a doorway. The door is closed. It seems heavy from the outside, with strong black iron hinges and two window panes at head height with images of sailboats imprinted on them. You can almost see inside, except you can't. You have no idea *what* is on the other side. Not one clue. And you're about to open that door and make a discovery.

Now notice, what are you feeling? Are you excited? Nervous? A little bit of both? Maybe life has been tough lately and you're feeling a little jaded? Or protective? Doesn't matter. Write it down. No judgement. No shame. Just the truth.

Me? I've always loved doors. I get curious. What's behind there? What kind of world will I walk into when I turn the handle and step through? (Can you tell I'm a big fan of CS Lewis?)

Ireland was a doorway for me. One I chose to walk through. So many of us spend time tarrying in doorways. Wondering should I walk through, or should I walk away and try another? Don't tarry too long in the ones that present themselves to you. Life is waiting for you, on one side or the other. As much as I love them, life was not meant to be lived in doorways. And if I had, Retreat to Ireland would never have begun.

Boys

"I feel this longing in me

It's like I'm wet and wild and tossing

But I'm normal, walking, living

My heart yearns. It does.

Mine and everybody else's."

-Kat Koch

Because every book should have a section on them. And because I entered Ireland having just left a long-term relationship only to experience unrequited love and then, eventually, start dating. The process of opening up again was mind-blowing.

Mom, please skip this section...

45

The Irish Republican

When I started running my Ireland retreats regularly I built a WordPress website to spread the word and inspire people to sign up.

Like most websites, I had a contact page. And like most contact pages, I received spam. One night an email came through from someone called The Irish Republican. The subject line simply read – Wow.

When I read the email, I instantly felt creeped out! Who was this guy? And how did he think it was okay to contact me and say such things?

I know this isn't politically correct, sensitive or upwardly feminist, but if I'm honest with myself (and you), looking back, what I mostly feel like doing now is laughing. I can appreciate his honesty and all his compliments. I'd prefer them from someone I know well, not a stranger, but hey! Life is short.

The email read as follows:

(No punctuation, phrasing, or grammar has been changed)

"*Kat, your body is amazing your ass is just out of this world. I would love to see that beautiful frekley face scream with satisfaction as I make you orgasm over and over, I'm only 22 but I would love to make passionate love to you for days on end you have the most beautiful curves I've ever seen such a woman. Hope your single*"

46

John versus the Irish Bouncer

He kissed me in the elevator, moving my long red hair away from my face to put his lips on mine. And I wasn't sure how I felt.

He was sexy, no doubt. We'd had an amazing night of live music, dinner, and parties. I just felt slow to warm. Even after a most hilarious (at least to me) incident between this beautiful black man I found myself in the elevator with and a 50-year-old Irish bouncer at the Metropole Hotel in Cork City.

I want to tell you what happened between them, but first, I want to give you a little *John context*. I met him back in 2014 at one of my gigs in Seattle. We really hit it off, like genuine good vibes between us. So we exchanged numbers and got connected on social media. I visited him in New York before I moved to Ireland. And now, years later, he happened to be in Cork City, playing drums for Cassandra Wilson during the Cork Jazz Festival. He invited me to be his guest for the night and I drove myself up from West Cork to meet him.

It was one of the most experimental gigs I've ever been to. The concept was amazing – exploring the connections between jazz and Irish music live on the stage. However, Cassandra's band had a delayed flight, lost baggage, and had barely made it in time to perform, let alone rehearse. The gig ended about an hour after it started. I'll never forget this Irish woman in front of me. She was texting her husband, and I could see the words on her screen.

HER: The gig is over

HIM: Already? That's the shortest gig on record. How was it?

HER: It was .... interesting

Cue my laughter.

Afterward, John took me out for dinner at this great little restaurant on Oliver Plunkett Street. He was an amazing date. Genuine and present, he actually asked questions and listened to the answers. Something I've come to realise is, unfortunately, not common amongst people, let alone dates. He complimented me. He paid for dinner. He was a total gentleman.

We decided to head over to an after-party for the artists at the festival in the Metropole. This hotel saw the start of the Cork Jazz Festival back in 1978 and was known for its great craic. So we walked and talked and wound our way down the streets of the city towards the river Lee, to its front door.

I remember the bright lights of the lobby glaring out onto the street as we approached. John opened the door for me and we walked in. An older Irish man with a distinct Cork City accent greeted us. He seemed a bit rough and ready, but friendly enough.

"Name please," the Irish bouncer said.

"John Davis," he said. "I'm one of the artists performing at the festival."

The Irish bouncer pulled out a thick roll of paper, crumpled from his jacket pocket, and started scanning the names to find it. We stood there for what seemed an eternity. In the privacy of my own mind, I was wondering how this man had a paper list in 2017! But then I remembered the first time I was pulled over by the Gardai in West Cork. Instead of taking my licence and going into his squad car, the officer pulled out a small notepad to take down my information. Right.

I could hear music coming from upstairs, it was swingin', and the lobby was busy with people coming and going. The Irish bouncer looked up from his manifesto. He did not have good news. No such name was on there.

Well my friends, what I was about to witness was a cultural standoff between two male egos. One, a New Yorker. The other, a Corkonian. Can you imagine it? New York versus Cork? What a standoff!

It escalated slowly when John asked him to take another look at the list because he was sure to be on there. I could tell from his tone of voice that he was just asking for what he needed and was being direct. Problem is, sometimes the Irish don't respond well to direct. I've seen it many times. It's almost as if direct means entitled to Irish people and it puts them on edge, bringing out their dry wit and donkey-like stubbornness.

I could see the tension building in our Irish bouncer. And as it did, I noticed John responding to it as well. They exchanged words. I stood, a witness to the male ego in all its glory, strength, and ridiculousness.

I'm going to be honest, this interaction fascinated me. It was as if the rest of the world disappeared between these two men as they exchanged words. Finally, John became so insistent that an Irish woman with an official badge (thank God!) came over and immediately disarmed the situation, encouraging us to enter through the backdoor of the hotel where they had the most up-to-date lists. I don't know how she did it. She was so calm and friendly – it put everyone right at ease.

When we entered through the backdoor, soft music, and candle-light were waiting for us. The new Irish bouncer asked for our names and pulled up John's immediately. On an iPad! It was the complete opposite experience from the brightly lit front door.

We walked up the stairs, bands around our black and white wrists, and got a drink. We had an amazing night. Like I said John was a great date. That's why I let him kiss me in the elevator. But I will never forget those two men standing across from each other like complete opposites, vying for their rightness.

47

Somebody Save Me

It was a normal, rainy Irish day when I met him. I'd just arrived at the job site off a tiny back road between Ballydehob and Skibbereen for another day of weeding.

On my knees, in the dirt and the wet, pulling little unknown plants from the soil. Digging out dandelions. And laughing with the other guys on the crew.

I looked down the driveway and a bunch of new men had appeared, circling around this big machine. It's strange, but one guy pulled my attention. They were covered in rain gear, so he didn't have any real defining characteristics. But I 100% felt drawn to him.

Throughout the day I learned that his name was Rossa. He was (and still is I think) a tree surgeon. And every moment he was on the ground, and we were near each other, we talked. I can't even remember what we said exactly. Mostly I remember a great vibe between us where the conversation flowed easily, and we kept sparking each other's interest. It was really nice. Especially because I was getting over an unrequited kinda love.

This went on for a day or two when I finally got a little heart and left him a note on his Jeep. It read like this: Want to hang out sometime? Kat (087) 755-6732

He called me that night.

Unfortunately, Rossa had a girlfriend. But the conversation continued that genuine flow between us from the job site. It was the best turndown I'd ever received! He told me he was flattered and then we tried to discover if we knew any of the same people, which we did. He said he was surprised we'd never met before now. It didn't surprise me though. My social life had become limited in West Cork. Mostly because I didn't know how to handle socialising in the smallest of small towns.

Anyway, when we got off the phone, I let the disappointment sink in. But I was mostly in awe of the nice way in which it had happened. And life went on. More weeding. More adventures. More Ireland.

Months later I was driving down the road when I saw a jeep that reminded me of Rossa's, and the memory of that day came back to me. The sexy tree surgeon in black with a girlfriend! Too bad it didn't work out, I said to myself. And on down the road I went once again.

Wintertime set in and I flew home to see family in the US for the holidays. Upon my return, I was super homesick. I'd begun to realise that I was having a hard time adapting to Irish culture, as much as I loved living there. I was also single. So single. And so struggling.

Imagine this now. A sexy single lady (that's me) is driving down a dark, twisting Irish road. She's sad. She's homesick. And she's a little bit lonely. She thinks of that sexy tree surgeon again because, well, who wouldn't? And in a desperate moment, she reaches out to the world with her mind and says, "Someone save me!"

She's immediately met with silence. And a few of her own tears.

Two minutes later though, her phone rings.

And it's Rossa, the sexy tree surgeon, calling.

I am not making this up. I looked down at my phone and his name appeared all bold in the lit-up letters and numbers. As the Irish say, I was gobsmacked.

I swear, sometimes it felt like Ireland was incredibly responsive to energy and intent. Things happened there that still defy my mind. Ask and ye shall receive, right?

"Hey, this is Rossa. We met on the river awhile back?" he said.

"Rossa? I don't know anyone called Rossa." I said jokingly.

He paused for a moment and when I told him I was just kidding, we both started laughing. We made plans to hang out that night. And I drove my big booty home to clean my room, shoving everything that was scattered left, right, and centre into the closet, slamming the doors. I changed my clothes but didn't shower. It's so funny looking back. I thought that would prevent things from going too far.

I'd been upfront and told Rossa that I had a quirky landlady and to be ready to meet that quirk when he arrived. But when I got home, she was nowhere to be found. That almost never happened. It was like an after-Christmas miracle.

Have you ever been called a sexy bitch before? No? Well, me neither – until that night. But first, dinner.

Rossa's jeep pulled up in front of the house and I went out to greet him. I was nervous. But kind of floored by the whole experience of his mysterious arrival back into my life.

He walked in, full of an Irish confidence I had not had the pleasure of meeting too often. That helped me begin to relax. I made us some tea and we sat chatting at the kitchen table. He had his tree surgeon cologne on, a mix of cut wood and diesel. I let myself drink in his smell as I sipped my tea. Two of my best friends at the time were tree surgeons and I'd always loved those smells.

He told me of his upcoming travel plans and I pulled out an atlas so we could track his journey. He was planning (and did indeed succeed) in riding his motorcycle from West Cork all the way to Mongolia. I remember meeting him over a year later and hearing some of his stories. About remote valleys, how his motorcycle was a tether to his own survival, and of course the magic of the people he met on his journey. This man had a lot of heart and guts and an ease with adventure. And I felt that crush wave begin to wash through me all over again.

Anyway, we continued to talk and as we talked, I made dinner. He was a vegan. I, on the other hand, was not.

But I didn't let that deter me! I'd been vegan once myself and never understood people who couldn't imagine what to fix for someone who didn't eat animal products – so many foods are naturally vegan! I pulled out the veg and olive oil and God knows what else and whipped up something tasty and forgettable.

As the evening stretched on and there was still no quirky landlady in sight we naturally migrated to another cup of tea. I went to put the kettle on and Rossa followed me. I turned around and he was right there, getting all close to my body and face and I knew he wanted to kiss me. He had already tried to get close when we were drooling over the map.

His body drew into me, and I paused to ask about that girlfriend of his. Turns out they'd broken up, which was a relief and a green light. So there, in my landlady's kitchen, Rossa the tree surgeon kissed me.

It was so passionate.

He turned me around and pressed his body against my ass. Later that night he'd tell me that he hadn't been able to stop thinking about me since the moment we met. That there were three things that really captured him. My laughter. My hair. And then he paused and tried to gloss over the third thing, but I already knew what it was. You either love it or hate it, that's how it goes with big asses.

As he rubbed his body against mine, I could hear the huskiness and desire in his voice and that's when he said it.

"God you're a sexy bitch!"

I later learned that this is a term of endearment in Ireland. In the moment I wasn't sure how I felt. A sexy bitch? Well, yeah, I guess I am! I just didn't expect it to come out of his mouth, a near stranger to me.

Slowly he started to take off my clothes, letting them fall onto the linoleum floor. In the back of my mind, I began to wonder how far I wanted this experience to go. And when I decided I wanted to stop, Rossa was a complete gentleman and blew my mind by doing something I've never had any other man do. He reverse sexy dressed me.

Take note of this, gentlemen who are reading now, this is a total turn-on. He kept making out with me as he pulled my thong up, my pants back on, and buckled my belt. Guy had skills!

No sooner was I dressed (though still dishevelled in spirit) did my landlady return. Impeccable timing all around. He and I excused ourselves upstairs to my room.

I've come to find out many things about Rossa over time, but here are two striking ones about him that I want to share. He is very honest, one of the most honest people I've ever met in general. But for an Irish man, he was incredibly direct and real. A fiery spirit.

He was also – what's the word? Warm. He drew people in. He was genuine. So, himself. I think it helped others feel comfortable in his presence.

Our journey as lovers and friends didn't end that night in my landlady's kitchen in Ahakista. But I will always remember him from then. How he appeared out of nowhere like a rough knight in shining armour and turned me on, both on the way down and on the way up.

48

#fantasy

I don't know what it was about him, but he turned me on. He was cute. Tall. Irish. And had an amazing dick.

Not too big. Not too small. Just right. Enough where you could really have some fun, but not so much that you were wincing or choking hard or working yourself up for it. It really was the perfect size.

The rest of his details shall remain anonymous because this is, after all, Ireland. I know any Irish person who's reading this is going to try to figure out his identity. And Ireland is so small they might be able to. But for the sake of privacy and a little bit of craic I'll just call him Goldilocks.

I met Goldilocks on Tinder and through a very strange sequence of events we eventually began hanging out. One fine spring day Goldilocks happened to be in my neck of the woods and he let me know that he was going to come over to my house and fuck me. I could feel his intensity through the text on my phone and it made me wet almost instantly.

I spent a lot of time with safe guys in my early years of dating. It wasn't until I moved to Ireland, started travelling, and started dating more openly that I discovered a whole new world of chemistry that rocked my own. And Goldilocks definitely did just that.

"Will you answer the door wearing lingerie?" he begged over text.

The next line simply read: *#fantasy*

This man is about 7 years younger than me. So straight up, he's a millennial. I'd never had someone hashtag me like that. It made me laugh! It also made me feel a little bit old. And damn it if it didn't turn me on.

I poured myself a G&T, turned on some music, and went into my bedroom.

I started by sliding on a set of nude, thigh-high stockings I'd purchased only a few weeks back. They were silky against my skin and the anticipation of what was coming began to build inside of me. Next, I put on a simple black thong and then a lacy garter belt to connect the stockings. I pulled a slip over my breasts and hips, put on some black and gold heels, and sprayed myself with Ellie Saab's delicious perfume. Red lips. Dangling earrings. And some more of that gin were the final touches.

He arrived not long after I'd finished. I heard the sounds of his wheels on the gravel driveway outside. I walked to the door, opened it, and let the cool Irish spring day pour over me. I had one arm up on the stonewall of my cottage and I was leaning against it.

"Is *this* what you had in mind?" I asked as he approached the door.

He didn't say a word. His lips were on mine as soon as he got to me. He kissed me into the house and up against the kitchen counters. I felt his hands all over me. I felt how much he wanted me. And I felt myself go soft between him and the hardness of the counter behind me.

He took me to my bedroom, and we began making out on the white sheets, the smell of gin on my breath, the smell of him filling my nose. Like aftershave and light laundry.

My panties were soaked by now and he knew it. So he slid his hand down between my skin and the black thong and put two of his big fingers inside me. Well, my friends, I lost my shit. Never, have I ever, felt so turned on by fingering. As the energy built I felt myself reach and raise and rise and suddenly I came. And then I came again. And again. And again. And again.

Five times I came within the span of no more than two minutes. And then I pushed him off me, stood up, and started laughing uncontrollably. Unabashedly. Laughing because it felt so damn good. And I felt so damn much. And, well, damn...

"Is that laughing a good thing?" he asked amused, a little perplexed and still totally turned on.

"Yes, it's a really good thing," I said smiling.

But he wasn't done with me yet. He pulled me to him and we began kissing, my tongue in his mouth, his lips insistent. And then, when I thought it couldn't get any better, he brought me to my hands and knees and entered me from behind with that perfect Goldilocks dick.

I'm going to be honest. I've had some *really* bad sex in my life. Like depressing sex, ordinary sex, distracted sex, running away from yourself sex, you know, the kind that makes you wanna leave your body and never come back kind of experience. Nothing violent. No rape. But nothing that made me think guys, or me for that matter, had anyone's pleasure but theirs in mind.

This was not any of those things. When I felt his dick inside me, filling me up in this totally fulfilling way, grabbing my ass and hips, I thought, so this is what everyone has been talking about.

Afterward, we lay together, talking. When he left I could smell him on my bed sheets for days. Aftershave and light laundry. I'd put my face on the pillow and draw that smell in, remembering every detail from the night. And I'd laugh.

49

I Think I Just Had an Orgasm in your Car!

Have you ever been so turned on by a conversation that you had an accidental orgasm? Without touching yourself? I have.

It happened one cloudy Irish day when my friend and I were in his car, driving between hang-out spots. I can still remember what he was wearing. A wool sweater, the sleeves rolled up a bit exposing his tanned, muscular forearms.

We were laughing. A lot. The conversation flowed so easily. Everything felt really good, and I began to feel all this pleasure fill my body. It was no secret to me; I had a big ass on crush on this man. But we were only friends.

The pleasure built and built and built. And as the conversation ended, I found myself squirming in my seat, torn between wanting to *allow* this feeling to move through my body and the unbelievable awkwardness at what was happening. It's funny, looking back, I felt like I had done something wrong. Now I understand that there is nothing wrong with my body's natural responses. There is absolutely nothing wrong with turn on, in fact it's a gift! It's just how I choose to respond to what's happening that can lead to some weird places.

Anyway, back to this unexpected orgasm.

I turned my head to look out the window and quietly let the pleasure wash completely over me. It felt amazing and afterwards I simply felt accepting of the experience, glad I'd kept the moment to myself. This man was a new friend, and I felt it best, given our dynamics, to leave what had happened unsaid.

Sometimes I wonder what it would be like if we were all a little more open, you know? What if we took things a lot less personally? Sometimes I wonder what would have happened if I'd told my friend that I'd had an accidental orgasm in his passenger seat. What if he'd laughed? Or got turned on himself? Or thought it was cool and asked me some questions?

This same orgasmic state happened again with him, only this time the distance between us was even further.

I was on an airplane getting ready for takeoff (all you dirty minds, quiet!). Suddenly I felt my friend as if he were with me, and a similar wash of pleasure came over me. It built and built and built and once again I turned my head and looked out the window! What was it with me and orgasms happening on transportation devices? Then he messaged me, out of nowhere to wish me safe travels and to see how I was doing. It felt like confirmation that he'd been thinking of me and somehow my energy felt his and did the most natural thing it could think of!

Fast forward a few months later. I finally did tell him the story of the time I had an orgasm in his car. First, we had an open conversation about my feelings for him and his for me. After taking in all the shared information we decided it would be best to be friends.

The air began to die down, a natural quiet filling his car. We seemed to have our most important conversations in vehicles, probably because we were always exploring West Cork, listening to music as we went. That's when I knew it was time. I needed to say one more thing.

"Can I share something else about all this?" I asked.

"Sure," he said, his consent given openly. I think he was feeling relieved about everything we'd just shared. I knew he didn't want to lose me out of his life and was grateful that friendship was an option.

So that's when I filled the space between us with that beautiful, awkward moment I'd experienced months before when I had the most pleasurable orgasm in his car. I'd already opened up to him about the accidental Kundalini awakening I'd experienced years ago, so he had some context for my increased sensitivity.

Let me ask you something. What if someone you cared about, but was still getting to know told you that they orgasmed in your car simply from the conversation – how would you feel? What would you think? I'm curious.

Do you know what my friend ended up doing? He laughed. He smiled. And he still wanted to be friends.

It was so freeing sharing that story with him. A relief. I mean, it's a lot to keep these kinds of experiences to yourself!

Kaleidoscope

"All the colours of the rainbow

Hidden neath my skin

Hearts have colours, don't we all know?

Red runs through our veins

Feel the fire burning up

Inspire me with blood of blue and green

I have hope

Inside is not a heart, but a kaleidoscope."

-Sara Bareilles

This is my gift to you now. Poetry, music, lessons learned, travel tips – both for Ireland and any special place you'd like to go. Oh, and how to come home. Because coming home after a life-changing experience is not as simple as you'd think. Whether you're an avid traveller or someone dreaming from their armchair, these stories are for you.

50

The Art of Arriving

You know the feeling, don't you? You've been planning a trip for months. Years sometimes.

You've read books and talked to people and scoured the internet searching for hostels and cafes and salsa dance classes. You've had dreams and journaled and stared longingly at other people's pictures of mountains, beaches, and horseback riding experiences. Then, one fine day, you finally take the leap and make the trip of your dreams. You travel to your destination, deal with any time changes, and start jumping into the adventure.

Only, you haven't really arrived yet ... do you know what I mean?

The moment of true arrival comes at different times for different people. When I lived in Ireland I met up with my long-time, American friend Andy. He was on his "Celtic Spiritual Pilgrimage" as he called it. He wanted to get in touch with his roots and, in a way, reclaim something he felt was missing inside him. So his generous wife stayed home with their child and he spent 3-weeks travelling, exploring, and journeying.

Andy told me a really beautiful story when he knew, deep inside, that he had really arrived in Ireland. He was in the Midlands exploring a delightful natural area by a lake where his ancestors once lived, long ago. He sat there thinking about his own family, letting his mind wander back and forth between Ireland, the US, and Canada. About the journey his ancestors took. And as he sat by that translucent lake he said he felt like he was finally, really and truly, in Ireland. That he'd arrived. And the experience meant something to him that I just can't put into words. It's something that needs to be felt.

I know this feeling too. I had it on my first trip to Ireland. It took about a week and a half of travelling before my moment came. I was standing on the edge of a set of cliffs near Baltimore, looking out over the Atlantic Ocean and little Sherkin Island. A white signal tower stood near me as the waves crashed against the rocks. The fields of green lit up my own green eyes and I thought, "I'm here ... I really am here!" Then I cried and laughed at the same time and the feeling of knowing I'd arrived filled me up.

One of the keys to arriving is using all of your senses. So the next time you smell a blossoming magnolia flower or taste a spice-filled bite of lamb tagine or feel the simple softness of a southwest breeze, really take it in. Allow your senses to be filled. This will help prevent home blindness in your own place *and* get you ready to fully experience your travels.

I believe *arriving* also helps you get into the mindset of what the French call *dérive*, another important part of travelling. It's the concept that even if you drift you will end up on the right path.

I love this idea. It's almost as if by drifting you are letting the magic in. And sometimes the magic needs that opening.

You've probably already experienced dérive. It's actually quite common. You know it, right? It happens when you're wandering through a new place and you just happen to walk down a path that takes you to a great discovery. Or gets you exactly where you need to be without you using your logical mind to arrive. It's like the art of arrival in that way. You cannot plan arriving. It just happens when it's time.

51

A is for Adventure: a Poem

Adventure is a rush. Adventure involves risk. Like walking in the woods on a wicked windy day. Or saying yes to someone you love with all your heart.

Adventure isn't always fun or safe or easy. But adventure is an amazing lover and sometimes, when luck is with you, can liberate you, exhilarate you, and bring on the fun.

Adventure teaches you about hidden aspects of yourself. Like a house with a thousand rooms, oh she takes time to explore...

Adventure is lively. And varies from person to person. Sometimes you need more risk the more you engage with Adventure. Less gear. Less preparation.

Adventure will leave you wet and sleeping in a ditch only to have you dine on pancakes with the mayor of Reykjavik the next day.

Adventure is a muse. She whispers:

Get up, move, see the sunset, find the key, kiss him (or her or them), satiate your hunger for life.

Then Rest comes in. Oh, welcome Rest. She gives you a hug and a warm nap in the sand.

Adventure dreams big and small. She does not care. What quickens your blood, she asks? Where do you feel truly alive? What are your hopes and dreams, and do you have the heart and guts to do your part?

"I'm not your mama," Adventure says. "I'm not here to ease your pain, per-se. I'm here to show you the world. How far are you willing to go?"

Take my hand

Breathe

Leap

Leap again

Rest

Repeat

Adventure just wants you to say yes.

But she's always clear:

"It's your choice," she says with her hand on her hip, "and yours alone." Then she smiles and turns on her way, as she always does, as she always will.

52

Call it Magic

Sometimes when I'm driving in a car full of people, I like to put my earphones in and listen to music.

I love the way it feels – being part of the group, but also being slightly separate, the music giving new meaning to the facial expressions and body language of everyone around me. It feels like everything flows together and there's less room for my mind to judge – suddenly I'm dancing without moving a muscle.

I also like listening to music in nature. I used to sit on Snave Pier in West Cork, back in the day when it was a quieter spot than it is now. I'd watch the waves move brown kelp, like lungs heaving. And the foam as it came sliding up against the rocks. The sea has so many moods – I think that's why I like her so much. I can relate.

Anyway, I'd listen to music and daydream. Relax. De-stress. And sometimes I'd get excited and kinda amped up by all the vibes.

My friend Cian and I shared a lot of music with each other during that time. We'd pass songs back and forth and each one we received from the other was like a little box full of jewels.

I remember one time I asked him, "How is it that you have so much amazing music?"

"Me?" he said. "You have the best songs!"

Since music was such a formative experience for me in Ireland, from listening on my phone to the pubs and live music events I attended, I wanted to create a playlist for you – so you can enjoy some of that music too. I've included 10 of my favourite songs, all of which I discovered or rediscovered during my time in Ireland. Of course, there will be a story for each. Listen! Enjoy! Pass them along if they touch you – music is meant to be shared. It's a language we all understand.

#1: "Sky Full of Stars" by Coldplay

The reason I remember this song coming into my life has everything to do with cherry blossoms.

I went to the Ballydehob Jazz Festival for a night of dancing and as my night wound down, I noticed a message had come in on Viber from *him*. My new favourite him. It was this song.

I put my earphones in and started listening to the music as I took the long walk back to my car – down the hill of Main Street Ballydehob and round the corner, past the old water pump, to the sea. As I turned that corner I was met with a breeze. It picked up all the fallen and loose pink cherry blossoms from a nearby tree and danced them down the street and through the air – a true spring wind.

It was magic.

The night grew darker as I approached the old railway bridge that crosses a narrow part of one of the water inlets of Roaringwater Bay. I walked underneath one of its 12 arches and towards the building that lies at the end of the road.

And then suddenly, light! The full moon was high in the early May sky casting its glassy brightness on the dark water.

"*Cause you're a sky, cause you're a sky full of stars, I'm gonna give you my heart*

Cause you're a sky, cause you're a sky full of stars, cause you light up the path."

#2: "All the Ways You Wander" by John Spillane

My friend Kenny and I were walking back to his car after our gig in the village of Clonakilty the first time I heard John Spillane sing.

We'd spent the evening in Molly's Wine Bar playing jazz and enjoying every moment. As we made our way back along the cobblestone streets of Clon, we heard singing and the sounds of a strumming guitar coming out of this tiny pub. As we walked past, I heard Kenny exclaim, "That's John Spillane!"

"Who's John Spillane?" I asked.

"Kat!!!" he exclaimed.

Kenny grabbed my hand and drew me into the pub. As I entered I could feel the physical heat coming off the people. Like sweat in the air. There was a man playing the guitar as part of a semicircle of people, some of whom had instruments. And we listened to a tune I've since forgotten.

It was John. Kenny told me that he was a well-known musician who'd found success in music later in life. Before that, he'd been an Irish language teacher! And that's what made me want to check out his music.

I found this tune on YouTube but really fell in love with it when I heard John play it live. I was attending his workshop on songwriting one summer in Bantry. He played it with such an open vulnerability that it's always stayed with me.

"All the ways you wander, all the ways you roam

All across great oceans, all across the foam."

#3: "Ireland" by Tori Amos

I'm pretty sure my friend Rosalee is Tori Amos's number one fan. She's loved her music ever since she was a teenager. You may remember, Tori even inspired Rosalee to write her second book!

When Rosalee, after years of having the inspiration, finally decided to come to Ireland for my retreat, she sent me this song. And when she arrived, we listened to it as we drove down the road from Kilcrohane to Ahakista in the moonlight. The car was full of good people, and it fit the moment perfectly.

When I hear it now it makes me think of her and the time we shared together. Man, I'm so glad she visited me. It's one of the best feelings in the world to share something you love with someone you love. Especially for someone like me who has friends all over the world. It's not common to have people make long journeys to come see the life you've created.

"Drivin' in my Saab, on my way to Ireland

It's been a long time, it's been a long time."

#4: "The Longest Time" by Billy Joel

When he said we should fuck him in the back, I went silent. My mind froze. Fuck him in the back? The phrase totally took me by surprise. This guy didn't seem like the kind of man who would want to fuck another man in the back of his van. I knew he must have meant something different, but I had absolutely no idea what it was!

Remember this story? Fuck was actually a verb and meant 'to throw'. He was trying to make a joke.

Not long after this moment, both of us laughing, "The Longest Time" by Billy Joel came on. We started singing as we drove down the road. The kind of singing that only happens with classic songs. It's such a happy memory.

I learned something else that day. Billy freakin' Joel sings that song! How did I not know that?

"I'm that voice you're hearing in the hall

And the greatest miracle of all

Is how I need you and how you needed me too

That hasn't happened for the longest time."

#5: "Can't Help Falling in Love" by Elvis Presley

Eileen's Bar in Kilcrohane is an institution. It's the kind of pub that holds on to times past, with whitewashed walls, old Guinness signs made of thick metal, and a peat fireplace that makes the whole place cosy. And hot, when people begin to fill her space.

My friend Kenny and I gigged there one autumn evening, bringing a jazz set that is rare inside those walls. My favourite moment was when we played "Can't Help Falling in Love" by Elvis Presley. I don't remember how Kenny and I chose that song to add to our repertoire. I just remember that when we did, we found it lent itself well to a quiet and emotional acoustic version of the original orchestrated song.

As I started singing, the pub went quiet. Irish people love live music and are some of the best and most honest to have in your audience. And as I'd experienced before in many pubs, when someone starts singing a ballad the entire place is shushed into silence.

When I came round to the second verse the people in the pub began singing with me, the half and whole steps of the ascending melody filling the hot air. It was one of the best feelings I have ever had while gigging. It was such a natural moment; no facilitation was required. Just a classic song in a room full of people who loved music and who felt moved, in the moment, to join in.

"Wise men say, only fools rush in

Oh, but I can't help, falling in love with you."

#6: "Magic" by Coldplay

We had just finished dinner in Kenmare when we climbed into his white van to drive the forty minutes back to our meeting place. Through the rock tunnel and then over the Caha Pass, with wide, reaching views of the landscape, its sheep and Bantry Bay in all her shades. The top of the Caha Pass has a wildness to it, even though civilization is not too far away.

As a foreigner, I really loved going to Kenmare. It had a more international feel and when the closeness of West Cork Irish culture became too much, Kenmare was a refuge.

As we pulled off down the street, he reached over to turn the stereo on, a CD spinning invisibly inside the sound system. And this song came on. I immediately felt it.

"It's called 'Magic' by Coldplay," he said.

This was the first song of theirs that I'd ever really registered and so began my love for Chris Martin. They've become one of my favourite bands. I used to have this fantasy that they'd come play a big gig in Ireland and then end up in a pub afterward and join a session. And as magic would have it, I would be there.

As his car turned corners and made for the straightaway out of town the song bloomed between us, the moment heightened by the music. How could something so simple as driving down the road with a new friend feel so amazing?

It's funny, there was this guy in Bantry, and we'd often pass each other walking down the street. Both of us almost *always* had headphones on. We'd taken to stopping each other and asking, hey, what are you listening to? He was always listening to something new and interesting. And for whatever reason, whenever I passed *him*, I was almost always listening to Coldplay! He'd roll his eyes at me and say "Kat" with a hint of loving disgust. And I'd laugh because I didn't care. You like who you like. It's much easier to simply accept it.

"Call it magic, call it truth

I call it magic, when I'm with you."

#7: "You Learn" by Alanis Morissette

When I started brainstorming this set of songs and stories, "You Learn" by Alanis Morissette wasn't even on my list of possibilities. I considered some of Alanis's other songs, but they just didn't feel right.

Then something happened.

I was doing a 30-day Instagram music challenge. I know, I know. Social media is everywhere these days!

Anyway, each day of this challenge had a different theme, and you'd pick a song that matched the theme. One day the theme was *"A song you'd sing a duet with someone on karaoke."*

And it got me thinking about this particular song. And how I'd totally sing a karaoke duet with someone on it.

I first heard it when it came out in 1995. My friend Beth and I used to sing Alanis's music in the car. And then, like many songs and artists from my youth, she disappeared and other songs and artists came forward.

A friend of mine in Ireland re-introduced me to her music. He told me that, as a teenager in rural West Cork, Alanis had been a saving grace, helping him to navigate his complex, emotional life experiences. I used to love imagining him in the mid-90s, surrounded by Irish countryside (which had an old-timey feel even when I lived there), rocking out to Alanis in his room.

So, I started listening to her music again.

The lyrics of "You Learn" are matter of fact and slightly rebellious, with a soft side. She's essentially telling us to welcome in all of life's experiences, because, well, you learn.

Life for me in Ireland was not always easy. At times I struggled with my mental health, which I understand now to be linked to my struggles with connection and community. And Alanis talks about all of this and more in her catalogue of music.

"I recommend getting your heart trampled on to anyone, yeah

I recommend walking around naked in your living room, yeah

Swallow it down (What a jagged little pill)

It feels so good (Swimming in your stomach)

Wait until the dust settles."

#8 "Strong" by London Grammar

Listen to this song when you're in an airplane that's descending and getting ready to land. The guitar line, chords and orchestration merge with the sight of flying through and then below the clouds, watching with anticipation as you get closer to your destination.

I'd never heard of London Grammar before I moved to Ireland. But immediately fell in love with Hannah Reid's haunting vocals. The band formed in 2009 in England and has put out 4 albums so far, the most recent called *The Greatest Love.* Their name doesn't have any deep meaning. The band just liked the words together. Their songs on the other hand? Definitely deep.

This particular song helped me get my power back when I found myself in an unhealthy relationship. One in which I'd followed my heart fully forward into, like a crazy person, like an artist. Only to discover so much illusion mixed with so much truth. Rainbow weather.

I used to listen to it and could literally feel my power returning to me. Like it spoke to the way in which I'd been duped by him. And by myself. Only it gave me a little bit more spaciousness, putting me in the position of having believed someone and in them, only to be fooled.

It was also around the time that I began to listen to this song intentionally that I went to Africa. I began to see and experience the raw power of nature, to spend time with actual lions, and notice how animals don't apologise for being. They. Just. Are. So, the lyrics hit home even more.

"Excuse me for awhile, while I'm wide-eyed and am so damn caught in the middle

I've excused you for awhile, while I'm wide-eyed and am so damn caught in the middle

I have a feeling, you're caught in the middle

And a lion, a lion, roars, would you not listen?

If a child, a child cries, would you not forgive them?"

#9: "Fiona's Lullaby" by Mason Daring

I heard this song before I ever stepped foot in Ireland. It's from the movie *The Secret of Roan Inish*, which inspired me to save up my money and go there for the very first time. I am forever grateful for this film.

Sung by Eilin Loughnane, a well-known Celtic singer from Dingle, County Kerry, its beautiful melodies are in the Irish language. The message is simple, her lyrics telling anyone who listens, little one, little one, sleep, sleep, beside my bosom, sleep, sleep. It sounds way better in Irish.

When I used to teach yoga full-time, I was known as the singing yogi at a couple of studios where I worked. I learned this one and it became part of my repertoire of songs for Savasana (final relaxation) at the end of class.

A friend of mine had a baby, a long sought-after baby. I remember when I sent her (and the babe) a voice note of me singing this song. I was at my friend Jean's house on the Sheep's Head Peninsula. It was a sunny day. I let all my troubles melt away and just focused on welcoming this babe into the world and giving my friend a lullaby to play for the upcoming long nights.

I think that's why I'm including the song here. Because the movie it comes from was a catalyst for me beginning a relationship with the island of Ireland. And because everyone needs a good lullaby in their pocket. For those stormy nights.

"Inionai, Inionai, Codailigi, codailigi,

Inionai, Inionai, Codailigi, codailigi. Codailigi, codailigi,

Cois a chle mo, cois a chle mo,

Codailigi, codailigi,

Socair sasta, socair sasta."

#10: "Rainbow" by Kacey Musgraves

When I left Ireland, I knew it was time to go. Now, when I look back at that time in my life, and when I talk about it, I tell people I was living an artist's life. Honestly, that's the best way to describe it. A life full of adventure, mishap, hardship, kindness, magic, travel, and an emotional rock bottom I didn't know was possible for me. I'm still recovering.

Sometimes my friend Tim would puzzle over me in a way only he knows how. He'd say tortured artists need their torture in order to create. It sounds bad when I write it, but he didn't mean it that way. It came out of his Gemini mouth and over the phone like lines of light phrase -matter of fact, understandable, real.

This song came to me towards the end of my time in Ireland. And the lyrics made me cry every time I listened to them, at least for a while. It fits the theme of this whole book. Of what rainbow weather is to me. It's about challenge and hope. And coming back into the present moment, knowing everything will be okay.

"Yeah, there's always been a rainbow, hangin' over your head.

Mmmmm, it'll all be alright..."

53

Relax and Feel the Next Approach

You're in Ireland. You're stoked. And you're finally seeing the verdant, patchwork green of wild fields lined with stone and hedge.

There are sheep everywhere. And your fantasy of meeting a ridiculously handsome Irish farmer seems closer than you've ever imagined. In your enthusiastic state, you have decided that you'll fit every single thing you've ever dreamed about experiencing into your ten-day trip. Day 1 on your self-made itinerary starts to look like this:

Leave Cork City and drive to Blarney Castle. Kiss the stone so that when you return home to your loud neighbour, you'll know exactly how to tell him off while simultaneously making him laugh. Then hop in the car and drive around the Dingle Peninsula. As you drive you'll stop and enjoy all the little villages and beaches along the way. Then end the day in Galway and relax with a pint of Guinness or Murphy's while listening to some live Irish music.

Sounds amazing right? And it is - if you have a couple of days to do it. But putting this schedule into one day? I'm just going to say it – INSANE. Don't do this to yourself. There's a pattern I've noticed when it comes to Americans travelling in Ireland. We try to fit a ridiculous amount of sights, experiences, and driving into one trip.

I believe there are two main reasons this happens:

1. We look at maps and say, "Hey, Limerick is only 62 miles away from Cork, that's not far at all!" And normally we'd be right ... except for one pesky little detail ... we don't know Ireland! The vast majority of the roads here are windy, narrow, and lined with hedges. Or rocks. Or sheep! So 62 miles ends up taking a lot longer.

According to Google Maps, it will take you (the bleary-eyed, fresh off-the-plane driver) one and a half hours to travel those 62 miles. I'd say, if you've never driven in Ireland before or it's been a while, it will take at least two.

2. For some reason, as Americans, we feel like we have to fill our time with as much as possible to get the most out of our trip. I believe that we have a culture-wide obsession with work, even during our vacations. Couple this with the reality that most people only visit Ireland once in their lives and the schedule packing begins.

This is a disaster for *most* people. There are some hardy souls out there with great travel companions who can do a marathon trip and thrive. But most will get fried by the end of their vacation.

You? You don't have to experience this.

Read on to discover what my dear friend told me and why it has become my favourite travel tip to share with people when they decide to come to Ireland...

Relax and feel the next approach...

I knew instinctively that this was a piece of wisdom I needed for my life and remembering this phrase has helped me on countless occasions.

Like the time I entered Ireland at Shannon airport after a trip to Berlin to see one of my friends. I often got nervous at immigration, even though my status was legal in the country. I decided to try this whole relaxing and feeling the next approach thing.

I walked up to the officer and he said, "What brings you to Ireland?"

I paused. I took a breath as he looked through my passport.

"Ah, I see you're living here. Very good. Okay, come through."

I smiled as I walked towards baggage claim to retrieve my luggage.

Relaxing and feeling into your next approach gives you space. And space makes room for you to actually see and feel what's in front of you. It also allows for more spontaneous happenings. If you're not on a tight time schedule then you can follow that mysterious sign you passed a second ago pointing towards an ancient graveyard. Or you can stay and spend some more time chatting with the local people you just met at the pub and take them up on that offer to call by their place later for a session. It gives you a chance to enjoy yourself. Ireland is a laid-back country. Go with it.

McCarthy's Bar by Pete McCarthy is a great book that will teach you the art of laying right back if you need some extra guidance. His stories are hilarious and they highlight many of the sights you'll see if you visit West Cork.

So, when you decide to plan your trip to Ireland (with or without me) and you begin to dream, research, and plan – keep my friend's phrase in your mind. Relax and feel the next approach. This is a great way to travel in Ireland and a good piece of advice for all those moments you want to rush through because you don't know what to do.

Let this be your travel mantra. Repeat with me:

Relax and feel the next approach

Relax and feel the next approach

Less is More

Less is More

We love space

54

Six Insider Tips for Enjoying Ireland

"The sun is setting in a burnt orange sky; the cliffs are black silhouettes; the sea, liquid silver."

-Laura Treacy Bentley

Travel Tip #1

Less is More

Just in case you missed it in the last story or are jumping in for a random read, "less is more" bears repeating. In the story before this one, "less is more" was called "relax and feel the next approach". When you have less to do, you have more space. And when you have more space, you can relax and feel into what the right next is for you.

Look, everyone has a different travel style. There is not one right way. But creating space in your travels can facilitate true enjoyment, sinking into the moment, surprising yourself, and decompressing. Ireland is the perfect place for this.

If you want to give this a try, but don't want to let go of planning altogether, take one or two days out of your trip and make absolutely no plans. When you wake up, take a moment. How are you feeling? What would be nice to experience today? What are you drawn to or inspired by? Then take that step and keep asking yourself these questions as the day progresses.

Travel Tip #2

Talk to the Old People

We live in an interesting time. Technology is fast changing both our inner and outer landscapes. But there are still people alive today who remember what it was like without a telephone or a television. They may remember travelling in a horse and cart or using an outhouse. And there are still people alive today, in Ireland, who grew up in stone cottages in very remote areas and never visited a hospital until their 90s. We are reaching towards this exciting and scary future while still tied to a slower, challenging, and beautiful past. This duality is very alive in Ireland.

I met an American in his 70s who had been living in Ireland for 45 years. He told me that when he was 14 years old, he and his brother hitchhiked from Pennsylvania to Kentucky on their own, and no one batted an eyelid. He said kids today get up to walk into the kitchen and their parents are telling them to be careful, there are dangerous things in there!

Listen

These kinds of conversations are invaluable, not only in your home country but as you travel. Old people, or elders, have so much wisdom, insight, and humour to share. Luckily, Ireland still tends to honour its elders. It is a great place to hear stories from times we can only dream about. Times that will never be again.

He had no phone

I met an Irish man outside of the village of Glengarriff who didn't own or operate a phone, of any kind. Remember, No Phone Joe? No cell phone. No landline. His sister had to write him letters in order to get in touch with him. One thing I noticed about this man – he had presence. His attention span was strong and I could tell he was listening. In a world where people are turning into goldfish and begin to space out after 8-seconds, this feels incredible.

So, talk to the old people. This travel tip should be pretty easy because old people (well actually most people in Ireland) will start chatting with you, especially if you're alone.

But don't wait for them. Do it now, before it's too late and their stories die with them. I believe we need to remember where we've come from as we move forward to wherever it is that we're going. Not only will connecting with an elder enrich your life, but also in the process, you'll honour the life of another. That is a worthwhile experience.

Travel Tip #3

Follow the Signs

As a curious American approaching an Irish signpost, I find I'm prone to a mixture of irritation and excitement. When I first arrive back in the country after some time away, it is the irritation I feel first.

I imagine Germans must also feel this. And citizens from other semi-organised nations. How in God's name am I to find the direction of what I'm looking for in that Christmas tree of a signpost?

But then again, I get excited. Dursey Cable Car? Glengarriff? The Beara Way? Hmmm... What are these exotic locales?

Sometimes you'll be driving along on a tiny excuse for a road in the backcountry of Ireland and you'll come across a sign such as this:

Burial Ground

I've come to realise one must, as often as possible, follow these signs.

One of three things will most likely happen:

1. You'll follow the first sign and then maybe another and suddenly you'll feel utterly lost as the road narrows and your heart

beats faster, so you'll give up and turn around. Especially because the signs can no longer be found.

2. You'll find it and it will be grand! A beautiful and unexpected spot!

3. You'll find it and it will be a dud.

Signs are Everywhere

But I'd say eight times out of 10 you'll be glad you took the time to venture off the known road and into the unknown, hedge-lined magic that awaits you. Follow the signs - you can interpret that as deeply as you'd like. But in Ireland, where men are men and the sheep are afraid, wait hold on, that's a bad joke from my friend Ger!

In Ireland, the faster you can leave behind your Western sentiments of order and knowing, the more you will get in touch with a country that hasn't lost its sense of right timing and ridiculous synchronicity and connection. Follow the signs. Just follow them, okay?

Travel Tip #4

Pick up the Phone

One July I got into a car I'd rented and headed off for the hills of SW Cork to go set dancing. As that strange half-light of dusk took over the roads, the hawthorn trees losing their jagged shapes, I jogged my memory for the proper turns along my route. The journey took a long time and an hour and fifteen minutes later I found myself outside of the Abbey Hotel in Ballyvourney – my first set dance of this trip!

Strange though, there were no cars around. And the hotel seemed surprisingly quiet. I walked inside and found the dance hall deserted, not a red-faced Irish farmer in sight. What the hell?

If only I'd picked up the phone...

Turns out that night was the *one* night a year the dance didn't happen. There was a big set dancing festival on in County Clare and everyone had gone there for the craic.

Ireland isn't big on websites and emailing, though that is steadily changing. They are into Facebook pages for businesses. And phone numbers. Chances are if you see a flyer for something you'd like to attend, the only way to get more info is to call.

I like to think that this is just another way the Irish keep their importance of people and connections prominent and avoid a culture of screen faces and entertainment. Or maybe they just can't be bothered, I'm not sure.

But it's pretty cool when you think about it. How often do we actually need to pick up the phone and talk to a stranger these days? The dentist? Yeah, maybe. When dating? Unfortunately texting is replacing an actual phone call.

Cellular or Landline, it doesn't matter

Picking up the phone while travelling in Ireland will help you get the information you need and may very well help you make you a new friend or get you invited to a party. It's hard to say.

In my experience, picking up the phone has gotten me lifts (rides, but don't say that in Ireland) to and from events, answers to burning questions such as, *"What movie set did I drive through last week?"* and spots in frigid yoga classes that everyone besides me was sweating in. But I digress...

The phone is your friend. Use a local one. Or get a local SIM card for your smartphone (this is pretty easy) and have your very own Irish number as you travel abroad. But do pick up the phone and enquire. You will get the most up-to-date information, and most likely a little extra.

Travel Tip #5

What do you love to do? Do it in Ireland!

This tip may seem obvious, but it's easy to forget while travelling. What activities do you participate in and seek out at home? Some of my most exciting memories and fruitful connections have been because of this tip. I met Sheila Ellis (who hosted my Retreat to Ireland for many years) by going swing dancing in Cork City. I met my friend Jean Williams (an 80-year-old woman who travelled solo all over the world) because of a Jazz Festival. And I had the chance to get to know my friend Dolf, all because I was dying to go to a Céili (Irish folk dance).

The Internet makes it simple and easy to search for events or meetings or festivals and find all those unique things you might be interested in attending. Or see Tip #4!

Seek and Ye Shall Find

Another great option is to go to a local tourist office and browse the flyers. I once found a flyer for a Seaweed Walk that led me to a day filled with adventure, including an impromptu tour of a mussel factory and an ill-attempted kiss from a 50+-year-old Irishman.

And, of course, just ask around. Is there some good live music happening tonight? Any hurling matches going on? Where's the best place to fish? At the very least you'll have a good chat with someone, even if you don't get a straight answer.

So, what do you love to do? Think about it. And when you're planning your trip (or planning on coming on a trip with me) let those ideas come to the forefront.

One thing to remember

When asking a question of anyone in Ireland, take your time. Have a little bit of the chat first before jumping in directly. You Americans out there need to be particularly mindful of this. Comment on the weather. Ask how they're doing. Take a moment. Then ask your question. It makes a difference, I promise you.

Travel Tip #6

Give in order to Receive...

Do you know what winsome means? According to Google, it was a common vernacular in the early 1900s. And according to the Merriam-Webster dictionary: *"Winsome: cheerful, pleasant, appealing, often characterised by having a child-like quality"*.

Travelling is a cultural exchange. Not only are you soaking in the essence of a place and its people, but you are also bringing your culture with you! Travelling is not a one-way street. It is an energy exchange, in its best form.

While on the road consider bringing something along to share. It could be a song, a favourite recipe, your knitting needles, or three of your favourite jokes. It doesn't have to be elaborate. Just bring something to share and share it *winsomely*, like a child.

During my 2014 Retreat to Ireland experience, we were very lucky to attend a cultural night near the remote village of Kilcrohane on the Sheep's Head Peninsula. Locals told stories, both personal and mythic. Musicians played and people danced.

And beautifully, each one of us from the retreat shared as well. I sang a song and two sisters sang their familial version of Happy Birthday in honour of their grandmother's birthday.

Another spoke about how touching it was to witness this event and be a part of the community celebration. As I said, we all shared and there was power in that.

For some reason, in America especially, we are taught that you have to be "the best" in order to perform. Most of the rest of the world doesn't feel this way. So bring something along with you to add to the vibe. Get out of the "entertain me" mindset and become part of the entertainment!

55

What Ireland Taught Me

Polarity is the death of subtlety and nuance. Black *or* White. Right *or* Wrong. Catholic *or* Protestant.

Polarity does bring with it a healthy dose of certainty. And protection. But the experience of life, if I'm really honest with myself, is more multi-layered than polarised. More complex than clear. Like a kaleidoscope. And Ireland is made of that kind of fabric.

Ireland taught me to hold complexity. To juggle it. In a much deeper way than I'd experienced before. It challenged my upbringing and sense of identity. In a way, it reorganised me. Changed me. And I will never be the same.

As John W. Gardner wrote, "Life is the art of drawing without an eraser." And Ireland was my most wild sketching yet...

As you'll soon discover, not all my life lessons were hard. Some were like gentle breathing. Or a 30-second pattern interrupt. Like fencing. Or a deep, dark pool. I like to imagine these lessons moving through my life like clouds that come and go. They remind me that there are plenty of options when it comes to how we live our lives and that ultimately, for me, polarity is a stage or a moment, while complexity is more the dance.

The 50 / 50 Principle

I wish I could show you my calendar before I travelled to Ireland for the first time. It was absolutely packed, like a peanut butter and jelly sandwich, with too much sticky peanut butter. Lines of colour ran across its grids. Filled with friend dates and date dates and work and appointments. It was by no means a boring set of events. It was full of delight. But it was *full*.

Next, I'd show you my calendar post Irish travels. The coloured lines began to disappear and within each box, there was, well, a lot of space.

I did this on purpose.

I'd been to Ireland twice by then, over the course of 9 months. Each trip had so many surprising adventures, adventures that happened because I was in the present moment. And these adventures were better than I could have planned. This new form of letting go and allowing life to happen, to touch me, to move me, was something I'd always longed for, but didn't know how to let happen.

My own unravelling of the tight life grip began before Ireland when I moved to Washington state and started learning about the natural world. Through my experiences with Wilderness Awareness School studying nature I began to taste this newfound freedom. And I loved it. I just didn't know how to apply it to the bigger picture of my life and my long-time, secret desire to be a full-time traveller.

It was the people I met on my first two trips to Ireland and the unexpected adventures we had, some of which led to new friendships and partnerships, that began to give me the confidence to let go on a deeper level.

And then, my 29th birthday happened. I had plans with my family in the afternoon, for lunch and a party. But I wanted to get out into nature and have some time alone. I woke up early and headed to my favourite Metro Park in Columbus – Highbanks. It was winter with plenty of snow on the ground and lots of fresh tracks. I decided to let myself wander, and go where I was drawn, with no particular outcome or destination in mind.

I'd learned a technique on how to do this at Wilderness Awareness School. It was called Radar Hands. You stand with your palms facing out, away from your body, and move in a circle, feeling which way you want to go, as if your hands are like antennae, drawing you towards something really cool. I'd heard stories of people finding rare wildlife this way.

But today, I simply followed my curiosity. Ooooh! Look at those tracks, I wanna follow them. Wow, that tree is amazing, I'm gonna go have a look. And since it was winter, all poison ivy and ticks dormant till Spring, I felt free to roam the hardwoods of central Ohio.

Donned in a green wool sweater, my breath making fog, I was having an amazing time. Eventually, I found a set of fox tracks in the snow, at the edge of an area I'd never been to. I began to follow the narrow trail down a small hill into a ravine when I looked up and saw what I thought was a dash of grey in front of me. I'd spooked some kind of animal, bigger than a squirrel, smaller than a coyote, and caught just a glimpse of its escape. Grey fox sprang to mind – an animal I'd been dying to see (they climb trees!) but had never had the fortune of finding before.

I could feel my excitement build and I wanted to run after it. And then, for some reason, I looked at my watch. Drat! It was time to turn around or I'd be late for family time. I felt completely torn. Between my plans and the present moment. And then I started to laugh. I called my mom, told her I would be about an hour late, and then went off in search of that grey blur. I never did confirm if it was a grey fox. But that's okay. More memories to be made somewhere down the line.

It really hit me that day when I struggled between my want for plans and my want for freedom. And that's when I finally discovered that I was a 50/50 woman. 50% planner, 50% sans plans. My time living in Ireland confirmed this. To float on the wind, letting life take me where it wanted full-time just isn't my vibe. But a part-time floater and responder? I'm all in. I learned that I do love creating and executing plans, it's super fun. And I've discovered that I can leave room for spontaneity within a structure, something I incorporated into the retreats I ran in Ireland.

On the Importance of Humour

As the sun began to sink lower towards the horizon, constantly shifting the colours and feelings of the Irish landscape, my friend and I drove to a very special place by the sea. Normally he drives, but that night, I drove. He told me a story about a quick-witted conversation between some people he knew. It went like this:

"Hey man, what's up?"

"The ceiling." (Man was being a wanker)

"No, I meant what's up your hole?"

Can you see the strange and wonderful genius in this? It's scary how fast Irish wit is. The first question was asked in a genuine way. When the second man replied with nonsense, the first question was easily twisted into a funny and jabbing return.

Irish people are fiercely independent in parts of their nature. They can spot lies and bullshit from a mile away. It's uncanny. I won't get into the why of this, I'll let you mull that one over for yourselves. On a bad day, their humour seems to be this magical and biting defence mechanism. On a good day? Be prepared to pee your pants with laughter.

I once heard a great quote that, having lived in Ireland for over four years, rings true: "*Irish diplomacy – the art of telling someone to go to hell in a way that they'll look forward to the trip.*" -Author Unknown

All of this laughter and wit and words got me thinking. Coming to Ireland (especially as an American) is like going to humour reform school. We, the offenders of slow wit, take on Irish tutors to help us grow and sparkle and jab with the best of them. It's a slow process. But I'll give you a tip on how to begin.

When you want to get angry at a situation, get funny instead. If you can't think of a joke, at least acknowledge that a joke could happen.

Here's an example.

Many summers ago, I was heading back to America after another 8 weeks spent in Ireland. I'd had an amazing time and was feeling relaxed and happy.

As I waited in line to check my bags at the airport, a man in shorts and funny socks came out of nowhere and stepped in ahead of me. In the US we call this sneaky act 'ditching'.

There was an American couple behind me and though I couldn't see the woman, I could feel her irritation radiating forward towards the ditcher. Soon she spoke up and pointedly told me NOT to let him get away with it. Her irritation grew, but all I could think was, "Shit! I wish I could think of a joke right now."

I could feel a smile growing across my face. And then the funniest thing happened. An airline attendant came over to help and without hesitation took me and no one else to the next available desk.

A Little More on Spontaneity

Tony Robbins, a famous life and business strategist, says that as humans, we need certainty. But in equal measure, more or less so depending on our taste, we conversely need uncertainty. Survival guaranteed equals a relaxed nervous system. Survival guaranteed for too long equals potato chips and a long snooze on the couch.

In other words, survival guaranteed for too long = boring. Stuck.

Enter Spontaneity. Goddess of ease and luck. If you're of German descent you might not like her. She ruins plans. Sometimes she enhances them, but often she takes a mighty sledgehammer to your day. You can be left with rubble or butterflies; it all depends on you.

Spontaneity loves Ireland. A lot. Here follows a comparison:

1. I met a couple from Philadelphia in the Bantry House Gardens in West Cork. I asked the woman where she was from and after her response went to continue the conversation by telling her where I was from. After I finished, she remained silent, and we parted ways. Very awkward. It didn't feel good at all.

2. Same location. My friend Ger from Cork City had some Irish kids minding his Parsons Jack Russell while we had tea. The kids (and their adults) fell in love with Scamp. When we emerged from the tea house, we had a long chat with them all, took pictures, and exchanged email addresses. Way more fun. Granted a dog was involved. But it had more to do with the nationalities than the cuteness of Scamp.

This kind of thing happens all the time in Ireland. The people there have time for you. They may not make their appointments on time, but for Christ's Sake, is it the end of the world? Of course, every culture has its shadowy side. I'm not idealising Ireland. I'm just saying it's some good medicine. Spoonfuls of Spontaneity every day would do most people I know quite a bit of good.

And to all my American readers, a note: Please don't be a jackass while travelling. Take the time to get to know people. Open yourselves up and stop being so awkward. You're pissing me off.

Life is not a Performance

Sometimes I have these profound waking visions. They happen during meditations. But sometimes they happen when I'm living, walking, breathing.

This one happened while I was driving.

Out of nowhere, it came, an unintended daydream. I imagined myself straddling one of my guy friends in Ireland. It was so sexual and sensual. I ran my hands over his head, and we moved together, facing each other, so close. I felt this rush of energy in my throat, like a waterfall of warmth and connection and my friend said to me: *Life is not a performance.*

I began to cry. Hot, wet, fast tears of knowing.

It felt like, at least some parts of me, had been putting on a show my entire life. So people would like me. Help me. Protect me. So I'd fit in and be accepted. So I could compete and get opportunities.

When those words fell out of his mouth in the daydream, I felt so much pleasure fill my body. Like a giant weight had been lifted off me. It felt like I might have a chance to be authentic. If I'd allow myself.

When I was about 12 years old, I was diagnosed with lymphocytic thyroiditis and later with Hashimoto's disease. My thyroid slowed down and then eventually began to spike and plummet. Needless to say, especially as an adult, feeling beautiful energy in this part of my body wasn't common.

Not long after this experience I found a quote by Marion Woodman, and it put so much into perspective:

Deep rage is not about the man;

Deep rage is this:

Nobody ever saw me.

Nobody ever heard me.

As long as I can remember, I've had to perform.

When I tried to be myself, I was told, "*That's not what you think, that's not what you ought to do.*"

So, just like my mother and her mother, I put on a false face.

My life became a lie.

That's deep rage.

Somehow, all of this feels connected. And I'll never forget that moment, driving down the road in the dark. It felt like the beginning of something that, for me, has taken quite a while to unfold. It is still unfolding. Life is not a performance.

56

Tips for ♀ Travellers

I used to get random emails or phone calls from my mom. She was the director of the Foreign Language Center at Ohio State University and a French teacher with a Ph.D. (go mom!).

Sometimes she'd meet with young women who were interested in doing a study abroad program and combining it with travel. And my mom, being the kind woman that she is, told them all about me and my adventures. Then, she'd give them my number or email address and tell them they could reach out if they wanted advice. Many of these women felt the draw to travel, but it was combined with fear and a certain kind of pressure to figure out what they wanted to be for the rest of their lives and devote their time in Uni to that answer.

I felt for these women. As a young person myself, I'd wanted to travel so badly. In high school, I used to watch the Travel Channel constantly. Back in the late 90s the Travel Channel was new and commercials only happened between their programming. I'd sit for hours learning about Greece from Rick Steves or a show about Eastern Europe and all its treasures. I was hooked. My best friend Beth and I decided to backpack around Europe when we graduated from high school. We made a massive binder of all the places we wanted to go and ideas of what to do and see while we were in each place. Thing is, we never ended up going. Finances, college, and safety all played into our decision.

Luckily, I did get to travel. But my travels started later on. Upon reflection, I realised a few simple things that, had somebody told me, would have made the leap to travel much easier.

encouragement

[in-ker-ij-mint]

noun

the action of giving someone support, confidence, or hope

use it in a sentence

"The encouragement I received from my friends and family made me feel on top of the world, like I could do anything!"

Sometimes all we need is a little bit of encouragement. Someone to say, you got this. I'm here for you. Take the leap! Enjoy the ride. And if you ever run into trouble, you can call me, here's my number.

If you feel that urge, that desire, that wanderlust to travel, I highly recommend you follow it. Give yourself permission to take a year off between high school and college. In fact, give yourself permission anytime you feel like you want it. Taking time off like this won't ruin your life. Do you know how many rich and famous entrepreneurs didn't follow the status quo, followed their dreams, and changed the world? Tons of them.

Steve Jobs, Sylvester Stallone, John Spillane, Sheryl Crow, Leonard Cohen. And my client Kyle Gray. He was a high school dropout (because of an incredibly discouraging teacher) and went on to create a million-dollar business that touches thousands of lives. Just because you go to college does not determine your success in life. So give yourself some breathing room and go out and explore! I promise you won't regret it.

waitress

[way-tress]

noun

a woman whose job is to serve customers at their tables in a restaurant

use it in a sentence

"My tips were so good as a waitress I was able to fund my travels!"

I wish I had thought about taking up waitressing way before I did. As a waitress I made between $25 - $30 per hour, which allowed me to save money easily. I wish someone had told me when I was just out of my mother's house, that waitressing was a completely viable option for funding my travel desires as well as my desire to live an extraordinary life.

I guess nowadays we're de-gendering the term. So, whether you want to call yourself a server or a waitron or anything related to waitressing, I recommend this source of income. Find a restaurant that values its employees and treats them well. You could end up having friends for life and a job when you return from your travels! The restaurant industry has a high turnover rate, so places are constantly needing new staff.

safety

[sayf-tee]

noun

the condition of being protected from or unlikely to cause danger, risk, or injury.

Use it in a sentence

"I've always wanted to travel, but sometimes I'm worried about my safety. Will I be okay?"

Safety is an important consideration when travelling solo as a woman. All travel comes with risk. To put it simply, this is true because living life comes with risk. Danger is unavoidable when you are made of skin and bones. But add ovaries to the mix? The potential risk is heightened, especially if you're travelling in more male-dominated cultures with very different norms to your own.

Research is your friend here. Knowing cultural norms and laws can help prepare you for what you'll encounter and assist you in your decision-making processes when you're on the ground.

Options are also a part of staying safe. When you have more options you're less likely to make poor decisions that could lead you into situations that don't actually feel good. Making sure you have enough money for your travels will expand your options and help keep you safe.

And then, there is trusting your intuition. This is harder to write about, but very important to consider as you begin to take more risks and explore the world. Everyone feels their intuition differently. I even know people whose intuition comes to them in the form of thoughts, not feelings at all!

The best way to begin to discover your own unique intuitive language is to collect stories where your intuition is confirmed.

Here are a couple of examples from my own life:

+ I felt the pull to go out to a trail I rarely ever went on. It's funny looking back, it literally felt like something was drawing me to that spot. Like I had to move. I ended up having a really magical experience with a friend who also "happened" to be out on that same trail. Had I not followed the pull, we never would have connected in that way.

+ I was living in Ireland and wanted to find someone to sublet my apartment for about 6 months so I could travel. A friend invited me to their party one day. I almost didn't go. I wasn't a huge fan of West Cork parties. But something in me said to head out that night. I ended up meeting the woman who would sublet my place and it was the perfect fit. Like seriously I couldn't have made that happen more smoothly.

+ One day I was on my Safari Guiding course in the bush of South Africa practising my guiding and driving skills with my small group. I decided to take them to a spot that was far from where we were. When you need to drive longer distances with your guests you can't talk to them as much or stop to look at things along the way, so we were taught to give them a cool animal to look out for to help keep them happy and engaged.

As we drove I got this little intuitive hit, a small knowing, I felt "White Rhino". When I looked around, the habitat did indeed seem like white rhino habitat; very shrubby and protected. Just as I was about to ask my guests to keep an eye out for them, we rounded a small curve and a mother and baby white rhino were crossing the road in front of us.

How does your intuition speak to you? When has it led you to something so perfect? Or kept you safe from a potential hazard? Write down everything and start to track it.

More on Safety in Ireland

In general, Ireland is a very safe country. I once left my purse at a pub on Cape Clear Island. It took me a while to get back and when I did my purse was sitting exactly where I'd left it. Nothing was missing. And a man sitting at the table next to it said he'd been keeping an eye on it.

In most places you can walk home from the pub alone at night. You can hitchhike. And pickpocketing isn't super common.

That said, there are some surprising safety concerns that you might not have guessed.

If you like to hike, Ireland has proper mountain conditions and weather changes quickly so you must be prepared. Bring layers, snacks, water and make sure you read ahead about your route. Ireland is notorious for having sparsely marked trails.

Another great safety tip is to not rely fully on your phone for directions. It's still quite common to lose cellular reception in Ireland. Download any maps you might need or better yet, invest in a topographic map of the area you're exploring once you arrive. You can usually find them in petrol stations. They are beautifully detailed and have ancient sites on them.

resources

[rē-sor-siz]

noun

a stock or supply of money, materials, staff, and other assets that can be drawn on by a person or organisation in order to function effectively

Use it in a sentence

"There are so many amazing travel resources on the web these days. But don't forget about the resources available to you beyond the internet. In your day-to-day life. In libraries, from neighbours and through your own experiences and observations."

Here are three of my favourite, lesser-known travel resources for you to explore your options, connect and get good advice.

1. World Wide Opportunities on Organic Farms

https://wwoof.net/

What is WWOOF?

According to their website:

"Worldwide Opportunities on Organic Farms (WWOOF) is a worldwide movement to link visitors (WWOOFers) with organic farmers, promote cultural and educational exchange, and build a global community conscious of ecological farming and sustainability practices. WWOOF started 50 years ago and has grown from a small group in the 1970s to a worldwide community of hundreds of thousands of people today.

As a WWOOFer, you will participate in the daily life of your host, help on the farm, learn about sustainability, experience a new culture and meet new people, and receive free room and board during your stay."

I WWOOF'ed in Ireland and I can tell you it was an overall amazing experience! If your communication skills are good, and you and your host are clear with each other, it's a great opportunity to get to know local people, try your hand at new skills, and have that unique cultural exchange they speak about. I highly recommend it.

2. Couchsurfing

https://www.couchsurfing.com/

While Couchsurfing as an organisation has changed a lot since I first used it, I still think it's a valuable tool and a great way to see the world on a budget!

Couchsurfing started in 2004 as a small idea between friends in Iceland and has since grown to include over 14,000,000 members from over 200,000 cities across the world.

It connects people together in a couple of ways. Some people host travellers in their homes as guests. You usually get a room to yourself, though I have seen hosts who offer literal couches as beds. It's completely free and you rely on the goodness and kindness of humanity to have a great experience. Everyone has a profile, there is a search function so you can look up the countries and cities you're travelling to, everyone reviews everyone so if someone is being sketchy, it won't go unnoticed. Hosts usually feed their guests and take them on adventures as well!

Some people inside the community don't host, but have another label, "Wants to Meet Up". This allows fellow travellers to reach out to locals to meet up for coffee or a drink as it used to be called and make a new friend in a new city.

I met my friend Jean on Couchsurfing, and she became one of my longest friends in Ireland. I am truly grateful for this platform and have only had good experiences.

3. Girls Love Travel Facebook Group

https://www.facebook.com/groups/GirlsLOVETravel

With over 1.4 million members at the time of writing, this Facebook group is super fun! I've seen women helping other women out of travel challenges and nightmares, sharing itineraries and favourite places along with photos of their adventures. And, while I have yet to experience this, there are people on there who have met in person and become lifelong friends. It's a friendly space with good moderation and only the occasional cringe worthy post or comments.

conclusion

[ken-klü-zhen]

noun

the end or finish of an event, process, or text

use it in a sentence

"After all my travels, my personal conclusion? The world is made up of a lot of good people. And kindness is just around the bend."

I hope these ideas help you. I hope you travel, I really do. Make money, save up, trust your intuition, let yourself explore your desires, hopes, and dreams, and live a life that is extraordinary to you. As long as you're in integrity and alignment with yourself, you are going to have an amazing, life-changing time. And guess what? You're going to get scared sometimes. And that is okay. Keep breathing. Reach out to friends and family for support. I promise you, you're gonna be surprised, for as rough as the world can be, there are some truly beautiful human beings out there who will look out for you. You just don't know them yet.

57

The Art of Returning

I've been thinking a lot about travel lately.

As travellers we spend so much time preparing for our journeys. We research and plan and organise, often months in advance. Sometimes we learn a language. But frankly, how many of us spend any time thinking about our return home?

Travel is an art. But so is returning. Of the two, coming home is often way more difficult than departing. Why is this?

1. Reverse Culture Shock

If you've spent a month or more in another country and then return to America let's say, you are not-so-subtly reminded of our crazy pace of life and heavy consumerism as soon as you hit JFK. If you land in Seattle, the blow is a bit softer. I spent two and a half months in Ireland back in 2009. There were barely any Starbucks. If you wanted coffee, you made it at home. Stores didn't open till 10:00 am and often closed in the early evening. The roads were frequently small and windy, and people still stopped to chat you up pretty much everywhere. You hung your laundry out to dry on a clothesline like the rest of Europe. It was nice.

When I returned to the US I was greeted by audacity! The employees at JFK airport seemed especially loud and rude. My eyes were filled once again with the miracle miles of stores open 24 hours a day, 7 days a week. And the roads were filled with cars big enough to transport a 12-member Irish Catholic family. I'm exaggerating a little here, but it's true. Everything is bigger in America. Literally and figuratively. We have more space. More people. Just, well, more of everything.

As travellers we immerse ourselves in a different life, sometimes markedly different. Not US to Ireland different, but US to Cambodia different. Returning home we see our place with new eyes. Sometimes those eyes are appreciative and sometimes they begin to look more critically at our system of living. And this leads me to my second point...

2. You are returning as a different person than when you left.

This is an internal world shift. You've left home, gone out into the physical world, and experienced new places, people, and ideas. What a gift. When you return, you may begin to see and sense that the way your life was set up pre-travel no longer fits who you've become. Sometimes making the necessary changes to transform your life can be scary, overwhelming, and confusing. Why don't they talk about this in the travel guides??

The Art of Returning is a skill. Learn its ways and make them your own.

Way #1: A day or two before you return home – imagine yourself there.

Picture yourself in your home, apartment, or wherever it is that you'll be staying upon your return. Visit places in your mind's eye that are familiar. No need to make yourself who you used to be in those places, just bring your current self, there. Some people call this sending your spirit ahead.

Way #2: Say Goodbye

On the last evening of your trip spend some time saying goodbye. Make a conscious transition by marking this time. Spend the evening telling stories, being with friends, going to your favourite places. Choose something that is meaningful to you and do it.

Way #3: When you return, give yourself time.

Let's face it, most people don't like feeling uncomfortable physically or emotionally. Part of the *Art of Returning* is allowing yourself to feel what you feel. I'm not talking about self-indulgent bullshit; I'm talking about being real with where you're at. Know that it may take some time to reintegrate and that is normal and part of the gift of travel. We are forever changed. Let yourself be changed. And allow yourself the room to continue that process at home.

Way #4: Become a storyteller

Get your closest friends together for an evening of fun. Make food from the places you spent time in. Share pictures or videos. Tell stories. Ask your friends for stories from *their* travels. Make bringing your experience home a joy that infuses into the lives of those around you. You will be like a breath of fresh air.

Ultimately though, my dear reader, there is no right way. Especially when it comes to matters of the heart and soul. Your heart and soul. In my experience, they both speak in the language of resonance. Like the striking of a harp string, grabbing your attention. Like the vibrations of a chord series coming from a piano that cause you to tremble and shiver. They are beyond the mind. They are magic. And they will never lead you astray.

Sometimes you just need to move everything out of the way and create enough space to truly hear yourself.

And the more you create space and listen, the more you will return home to yourself. In your own right timing. You will unfurl. This is the Art of Returning.

Afterword

My own Art of Returning, the deeper returning to myself, has included a lot of Rainbow Weather. Like, loads. I've needed umbrellas and waterproof gear and a wetsuit as I went! I navigated familial and ancestral conditioning, cultural conditioning and challenging life experience conditioning.

I got lost. Really lost. Especially in Ireland. And for a while, getting lost was actually amazing. It led to unexplored places, reclaiming courage and the cultivation of trust, both in myself and the world around me. Until I reached a deeper level of lost, one marked with a kind of fear that still doesn't make sense to my conscious mind. The kind of fear that feels beyond personal.

I woke up one day in Ireland with a feeling I'd never felt before. I searched for the right word, rolling one and then another around in my mouth as I lay in bed. Sadness? No. Fear? No, not really. What was this sensation? Then it arrived like a bittersweet burst.

It was regret.

At that point in my life I didn't have a conscious relationship with regret. I'd always felt like life was a journey and all experiences were worthwhile on some level.

But then regret came in, like a gift. She whispered her message over my heart and I began to cry. I knew I needed a change. Because I didn't like what I was feeling. Obviously I'd missed the earlier messages.

So, I did as she asked. I changed. And that started with me leaving Ireland. My mind had been softening, especially through my travels in Africa and I realised that you don't tell a flower to change when it isn't thriving in the soil. You replant it. Or at least give it some fertiliser!

For a while, I put Ireland so far in my rear-view mirror that I swore I'd never go back. And I needed that.

I returned there in March 2022 for a trip with one of my longest friends and struggled. I didn't really want to be there, though I was so happy and grateful to be with her.

But the more I wrote this book, the more I remembered the whole picture of my time coming and going from Ireland's shores. I remembered all the deep magic that wove its way through my life. And I felt this overwhelming gratitude for everything that had happened. I started to be able to see the gifts. And let go of the rest. I think this is what they call integration.

In December of 2023 I returned again. To finish this book. And walk the landscapes that my heart loved so much. But you know what's funny? I didn't do either thing. The weather was shit and something happened that I didn't expect.

The loneliness I'd experienced previously in Ireland? Gone. My time was absolutely jam packed. And the magic and flow I'd once associated with this place returned. In fact, I didn't have nearly enough time to do everything I wanted. The morning I flew out on my way to Cairo, Egypt I felt so happy and full and excited to come back, in the summer mind you, for more.

The music, the people, the vibe, the conversations – they touched me. Ireland and I, we were starting to open up to each other again. And it felt really good.

xox Kat

Acknowledgments

Writing a book is the strangest experience! It's a deeply solo one, yet so interwoven. And this book is filled with the magic, love and support of both people and places. I have been lucky. Some might call it the luck of the Irish.

Lately I've been thinking a lot of my grandmother who passed on years ago, Virginia Kathryn Weaston. She was one of my favorite people and I loved spending time with her. She used to say I'd become a writer one day. I wish I could ask her about it now. Grandma, thanks for planting those early early seeds on becoming.

I want to thank my mom, Diane Birckbichler. You read my early drafts, gave love, encouragement and copy-editing suggestions, listened to me moan and wax poetic and cooked many a delicious meal on my visits to your home. Thank you for always being there.

To my cousin Julie Standish, thank you for your love and encouragement as well! You've been a part of the *whole* journey. I remember the first time you told me you liked one of my stories. It gave me the start of a feeling that someone outside of our family might actually enjoy this book. You always tell the truth and are a voracious reader and librarian – that's how I knew I could trust the feeling.

To my Gemini best friends, Tim and Beth, I love you two so much. Thanks for being there. For listening. For reading early drafts. Tim, thanks for making me laugh on the regs. And Beth, thanks for giving me Taylor Swift songs to torture Tim with. You are both chosen family.

To Amber Ault, I don't even know where to start! From our stars-aligned meeting on Aldrich to our Zoom calls from afar, your support has been a keystone on my journey. You introduced me to London Writer's Hour. You checked in with me regularly and supported me via Patreon. I don't quite have the words to describe your support. I am so grateful for you.

To my friend Kyle Gray, thank you for your support and encouragement over the years. You were the 2nd person in my life (my grandmother being the first) who told me that one day I'd write a book. You knew! How did you know?? You magic being, you.

London Writer's Hour, THANK YOU for continuing with your Covid experiment. Your daily writing sessions helped keep me focused, inspired and gave me a sense of community. So grateful for your team and the writers I shared space with!

Big thanks to Claire Gibson for connecting me with the writing room that would become home, Room 206. I found a network of sisters in all the women there. Thank you for being the bridge that brought us together.

And Room 206? Where do I begin! I remember the first time I walked into your former office in Parkhurst. My project was up on your wall and the beautiful, creative flow that we shared was present from the start. I remember leaving that day and thinking, wow, that was an experience! I love when people facilitate something *more* than just business.

To Natasha Fracchiola, founder of Room 206, thank you. While everything has shifted since we first met, I will forever be grateful for your love, expertise, creative soul and facilitation magic. Barcelona is lucky to have you.

To Robyn Porteous, thank you for being my first touch point at Room 206. I loved working with you on the 1st draft of Rainbow Weather. Your clear mind and kindness were so much appreciated.

To Leanne Crighton, thank you!! I'm so glad Rainbow Weather made you laugh and start to have a different vision of West Cork other than the podcast!! I couldn't have birthed this book into the world without you and your wisdom.

To Candice Burnett, thank you!! Thank you for keeping the big picture, drilling timelines into my soul and sharing your creativity with this project. I am so glad to now call you friend.

To Jamie Conway, thank you. You copy edited my entire book and I never met you once! Was so delighted to finally get the chance to share time together. You are a beautiful writer, and I can't wait to read your book.

Navigating the experience of creating and designing a cover for Rainbow Weather stretched me. For months I meditated, gathered ideas, looked at other people's books and put together a mood board with images that made me happy. I had this intuitive nudge to reach out to Megan Clancy from West Cork and I'm so glad I listened! Meg, thank you. The way you guided me through the process and were flexible with my feedback pace was very much appreciated. Thank you for creating a cover inspired by one of my dreams that is truly a piece of art. I love the way you work.

To my friends, Dolf D'Hondt, Bernie O Sullivan, and Kenny Dread. Thank you for being my "on Irish soil" question answerers. Dolf, thanks for trying to figure out the history of that stone! Bernie, thank you for answering my endless series of questions both big and small over Viber. And for hosting me as a singer in your beautiful space. Kenny, thank you for having me as a guest on my trips back, making amazing food, accompanying me on guitar many a night by the fire and for your thoughtful words on my project – you are appreciated!

Big thanks to my Kickstarter backers, specifically Briana Cribeyer, Deanna Tregoning and Diane Birckbichler. You three backed up the project BIG time and surprised and delighted my heart. I appreciate you more than you know.

And finally, to Nathan. You have inspired my words so many times. Thank you for soulful feedback, so much food for thought, epic cuddles and for sharing the kind of music that made me feel like we were on a journey even when we were just in bed.

xox Kat

P.S. One final thank you. Thank you to the natural world, Mother Earth, nature, all the names you go by. After my first year at Wilderness Awareness School, I felt this deep appreciation and connection to you. You have supported me every day before and since. I'm only more aware of it now. Thank you for your clear reflections, your grounding presence and the magic I've been lucky enough to witness, both right from the windows of my home to deep in the African Bush. I am so grateful for you.

Rest in Peace and Power

There are those who have passed away since the writing of this book. Those I want to take a moment to remember because they unequivocally touched my life. Perhaps you've experienced this too? If so, take a deep breath and say their names.

To Vernon Bellecourt who passed away on the 13th of October 2007, over 18 years after his words touched my life, thank you. Rest in peace and power.

To Maeve Gavin who passed away on the 13th of October 2018, I miss you. I can still see your shining face and blonde curls clearly in my mind's eye. Rest in peace and power.

To Pat Murphy who passed away on the 19th of February 2019, you are a very special person too. I'm so sorry we never got to meet again. Thank you for the magic. Rest in peace and power.

To Jean Williams who passed away somewhere around the 19th of November 2021, I will always love you. I miss you. Rest in peace and power.

And finally, to Val Manning who passed away on the 7th of December 2024, thank you for the wine, for the chats and for letting me smudge Manning's, even though you thought it was crazy. Rest in peace and power.

About the Author

Kat Koch boarded her first plane at two years old and hasn't stopped travelling since. She has been to 18 countries and lived in two. As a little, red-headed girl she used to tell her mom over and over again that she wanted to go to Ireland.

She finally made it. This is her debut book.